What's Next?

What's Next?

*How to Prepare Yourself
for the Crash of '89
and Profit in the 1990's*

Paul Erdman

BANTAM BOOKS
TORONTO · NEW YORK · LONDON · SYDNEY · AUCKLAND

WHAT'S NEXT

A BANTAM BOOK 0 553 175920

First publication in Great Britain

PRINTING HISTORY
Bantam edition published 1988

Copyright © 1988 by Paul Erdman

Bantam Books are published by Transworld Publishers Ltd.,
61-63 Uxbridge Road, Ealing, London W5 5SA, in Australia by
Transworld Publishers (Australia) Pty. Ltd., 15-23 Helles
Avenue, Moorebank, NSW 2170, and in New Zealand by Transworld
Publishers (N.Z.) Ltd., Cnr. Moselle and Waipareira Avenues,
Henderson, Auckland.

Made and printed in Great Britain by
The Guernsey Press Co. Ltd., Guernsey, Channel Islands.

To my wife, Helly, and our two daughters:
Conny, the spy, and Jenny, the banker

Acknowledgments

I would like to express my special appreciation to my old friend Clay Felker of *Manhattan, inc.*, who started the whole thing, and Patrick Filley, my editor at Doubleday, who so ably saw it through to the end. And to Doubleday itself, for moving at the speed of light, something highly unusual in the publishing business.

Furthermore I want to thank Jerry McGrath, Alex Trezesniewski, and John Connolly of Dean Witter Reynolds, Inc., also Clyde Pitchford, who provided the setting at Kapalua Bay where much of this was written.

Contents

The binge is over. It couldn't go on forever: the quick fortunes, the midnight raids and computer-driven program trades, the junk bonds, poison pills, leveraged buyouts, options—all the glitz and glamour, the danger and thrill. It's over.

—Robert B. Reich
John F. Kennedy School of Government
Harvard University

What's Next?

Introduction

FOR A WHILE IT LOOKED AS IF IT WAS GOING to last forever. From the summer of 1982 to the fall of 1987, the United States was on the biggest and best peacetime economic roll in its history. Unemployment, which had risen to levels as high as 11 percent in some key states in the union in the aftermath of Jimmy Carter, was in the process of sinking to eighteen-year lows in late 1987 under the aegis of Ronald Reagan. The stock market—oh, the stock market!—experienced its biggest boom ever. Between August of 1982 and August of 1987 the Dow Jones Industrial Average went from

777 to 2,722. And we were being told from all quarters —the stockbrokers, the economists, the White House— that we hadn't seen nothing yet.

I remember participating in an investment conference in late August of 1987 in San Francisco just as the Dow was hitting its all-time highs, sitting beside the Great Guru of the Bull Market of the 1980's, Robert Prechter. He's a nice man, studied the humanities at Yale, and is basically a market technician who believes that psychology, not economics, drives the stock market. He postulates that all markets move in waves, alternate waves of optimism and pessimism. And while I was sitting beside him on the podium in the Grand Ballroom of the Fairmont Hotel, in his soft voice he told the one thousand people in front of him (who were paying $600 a head for the privilege) that the next wave of optimism was upon us and was about to drive the Dow to 3,600.

Wow! They loved it!

Not a person in the room disagreed with him. We were all acting like that drunk who, as he keeps drinking, first believes he is invulnerable, then invisible.

Yet just sixty days later, the Dow had plummeted to 1,738, down almost 1,000 points. During those sixty days, the wealth of the nation was diminished by over one trillion dollars. Yes, $1,000,000,000,000 disappeared into thin air. And we blew half that much, a half trillion dollars, in just six and a half hours of trading on October 19, 1987. That's more than all the people of Central America plus most of the inhabitants of Eastern Europe earn in an entire year.

What the hell happened? Why did it happen? What does it portend (and, equally important, what does it *not* portend) for our financial and economic future?

1988

The Period of Grace

———————

One

Paradise Lost

THE MELTDOWN ON WALL STREET ON OCTO-
ber 19, 1987, was more than just a uniquely severe financial panic. It was a watershed event with implications
that went far beyond New York's financial district, for
the happenings that day finally shattered our illusions:

- the illusion that good times were here to stay;
- the illusion that prosperity could be bought in-
  definitely by the United States going perpetually
  deeper in debt;
- the illusion that, in the end, Reaganomics was
  anything but an illusion.

To be sure, the first thing it taught us was that the sky is *never* the limit on Wall Street. It brought to an end, or at least it should have brought to an end, the irrational belief that the stock market could completely ignore economic realities forever. Everyone told you that all you had to do was put your IRA money in the Magellan Fund and it would double, triple, quadruple ad infinitum, no matter what was happening in the real world around us. The new financial wisdom was that only a fool, like your grandma, would be dumb enough to leave her money in a savings account, getting a pitiful 6 percent interest. Nobody in his right mind, we were told, settles for less than 20 percent these days, and the real pros will get you 30 percent.

Who was selling this nonsense to the great American investing public? The professional money managers, that's who: the big boys in the investment banks in New York, Chicago, and San Francisco, and their little brothers in the brokerage shops in Peoria, Petaluma, and Paris, Texas. Up until the day of the Panic, this new breed of investment bankers, brokers, investment advisers, and newsletter writers was, almost without exception, telling us that stock prices were no longer governed by historic standards, or even by economic fundamentals. The key to your financial future could be found only in "Technical Analysis."

When you had tuned in to the Financial News Network in the summer of 1987, you were confronted with the new purveyors of voodoo. They sat there before the cameras, flashing their charts, pointing at some *computer-generated* squiggles, and telling you that a new "head and shoulders" was building, meaning, they said, that the Dow had to move up another 200 points during the next thirteen days. Do computers lie? Of course not. The message was not only clear but irrefutable: get into the market quick, before the new world of instant wealth passes you by.

So we squinted at the TV screen, and then picked up the phone and called our brokers.

"Buy," we told them.

"Buy what?" they asked.

"It doesn't matter," we replied. "I just saw Prechter on television, and he says the whole market's going up, way up. His computer agrees. So get some IBM, some GM, some Kodak, and, just for fun, some more Apple Computer."

And they all went up.

If we, for some reason, had second thoughts, all we

had to do was read *Forbes* magazine, or tune in Louis Rukeyser and his guests on Friday night. Nothing to really worry about, we were told, as the Dow went through 2,700. Sure, we might have a little correction now and then. But 3,000 on the Dow before Christmas is as good as a sure thing. None of them, and I mean none, even entertained the thought that we would see the Dow as low as 2,000 ever again. Ever!

And since we all *wanted* to believe, we did. It was as if wishful thinking had replaced rationality. For traditional analysis of the financial situation in the summer of 1987 would have led to a clear-cut conclusion: the stock market, as measured by the Dow Jones, the Standard & Poor's 500, or any index you chose to use, was way, way out of whack.

1. Stocks were selling at 22 times earnings.
    - The average historic P-E (price-earnings) ratio is between 12 and 13 to 1 (i.e., if a company earns $10 a share, its shares would typically sell for $120 to $130 each).
2. Stocks were selling at almost 3 times book value.
    - Historically, the norm is half that, or 1.5 times book (meaning that the price you paid

for the shares of an average company was 1¹/₂ times what you would get if the company was liquidated, everything from its land to its inventories sold, and the proceeds were then paid out to the shareholders).

3. The yield on the S&P 500 had sunk to the lowest level in recorded history, below 2.7 percent.

- The historic norm for yields is between 4 and 5 percent (meaning that you would typically get an annual dividend of $4.00 to $5.00, not just $2.70, on a stock you bought for $100).

In other words, every red flag was up, but we all ignored them.

The first flag of all, a yellow early-warning signal, had already been hoisted a full *year* before the eventual panic on Wall Street, and it had come in the form of the best and most reliable of all indicators of where things are headed: interest rates.

To understand their key significance and role in the Panic of '87, you have to go back to the fundamental reasons why markets move the way they do. It is my firmly held opinion that stock markets are not driven by squiggles on charts or pop psychology. They are driven by two basic forces: interest rates and/or profits.

Bull markets, then, have their origins in either

- falling interest rates

and/or

- rising profits, or at least the prospect of rising corporate profits.

Interest Rates and the Bandwagon

The Great Bull Market of 1982–87 was very definitely an *interest-rate*-driven market. It will probably go down in the records as an absolute classic in that respect. Thus you can pinpoint its origins: August 1982 and the resolution of the Mexican debt crisis.

The situation that existed in the summer of 1982 was a very dangerous one. Paul Volcker, when he was appointed chairman of the Federal Reserve Board in 1979, had inherited a highly inflationary situation, one that could have gotten out of control and that could have had devastating long-term economic consequences for the United States in the 1980's. The easiest cure in such a case would be recession. The way to initiate that cure: the government would have to severely restrict the nation's money supply. This would cause interest rates to skyrocket. That would strangle the economy and cause high unemployment; as unemployment rose, wage rates would stop rising, which, in turn, would remove the need for further price increases and thereby break the back of inflation.

That's precisely what Volcker did, with the tacit blessing of Ronald Reagan. He drove the prime interest rate to 20.5 percent, the highest level of the century. And it worked. Inflation collapsed. But America paid a huge price: the recession of the early 1980's was the deepest this country has gone through since the Great Depression of the 1930's. However, in the summer of 1982 it started to look as if the cure might end up being worse than the sickness it had been meant to heal. For all of a sudden it appeared once again that the economy might be on the verge of spinning out of control, but this time on the down side. The reason: on August 20, 1982, at a meeting at the Federal Reserve Bank of New York, Mexico's finance minister told more than a hundred American bankers who had gathered there that unless his country got a lot more money, in the form of new bank loans, Mexico was going to have to default on the huge debt, tens of billions of dollars, it already owed them. That could have led to panic withdrawals of funds from the most exposed banks, creating a liquidity crisis that could have driven interest rates still higher, maybe much higher (perhaps as high as 25 percent)— and, perhaps, turned recession into depression.

But with funds already so scarce that short-term interest rates were 20 percent and higher, where would the banks get the money to save Mexico (and themselves)?

Volcker provided the answer the next day: the Federal Reserve flooded the money and capital markets in New York with liquidity. But conditions were attached. If the Fed played ball, so now must the banks. In stepped Actor #2, Jacques de Larosière, chairman of the IMF, who called the representatives of all major banks to a meeting in Washington. He announced that Mexico's total needs were $8.3 billion. The IMF (International Monetary Fund) would contribute $1.3 billion; governments were contributing $2 billion more; and he expected the banks to kick in $5 billion, and what's more he expected it in a month. The bankers were stunned, but had no choice but to give in. A top man from Morgan Guaranty Trust Company of New York put it this way: "Jacques de Larosière's move was a major event in the history of banking." [For details on this turn of events, I recommend Susan George's book *A Fate Worse than Debt,* published by Grove Press.] Mexico was saved. Confidence was restored. The crisis resolved.

This shift in the monetary policy of the United States, from being highly restrictive to, all of a sudden, becoming extremely accommodating, was a watershed not only for Mexico, but also for all financial markets in the United States. From that time on, interest rates began to fall and the bond and stock markets—which had been stuck in the 750–900 range on the Dow for what seemed an eternity—began to rise. In speech after speech after 1982, I suggested to audiences that every time interest rates went down, the Dow would go up. It worked like a charm. It was almost automatic. Every time interest rates went down one full percentage point, the Dow Jones Industrial Average would go up 50 to 75 points.

The Great Bull Market of the 1980's was off and running. And this formula—interest rates down, stock market up—held until January 1986. That was the month that interest rates took their final plunge, this time compliments not of Paul Volcker but of Sheik Ahmed Zaki al-Yamani, the oil minister of Saudi Arabia. The Saudis had decided that they were no longer going to be the fall guys within OPEC.

Heretofore, every time the other members of OPEC got greedy and began pumping more oil than the world market could absorb, potentially undermining the price of oil, the Saudis would compensate by decreasing their output. By doing so, they kept the world price at about $28 a barrel. But they paid a huge price. For as Saudi Arabia's output sank from a peak of 11 million barrels a day down to 4 million, that nation's income—derived almost entirely from oil exports—declined drastically. As a result, the Saudi government was suddenly forced to begin drawing upon the huge cash reserves it had built up in bank accounts throughout the world, in order to finance a large number of domestic development projects that were only half completed. At the end of 1985 the Saudis had had enough. So in January they suddenly stepped up their output, a large amount of new oil surged into the world market, and the price collapsed—all the way down to $8.00 a barrel.

As the oil price collapsed, so did inflationary expectations and—so did interest rates throughout the world,

but especially in the United States. The bench-mark
long-term interest rate, that on the thirty-year U.S.
Government bond, the so-called long bond, fell from
9^1/$_2$ percent to 7^1/$_2$ percent, sometimes even 7^1/$_4$ percent
. . . the lowest levels of the decade. This, of course,
caused the stock market to surge yet again.

But then the first yellow flag was hoisted. Interest
rates got stalled. They stayed in the 7.25 percent to 7.65
percent range month after month . . . well into fall
1986. Had you gotten a little worried and called up your
stockbroker then, his answer would have been instantly
reassuring.

"Look," he would have said. "The world is awash
with liquidity. The Swiss, the Japanese, the Germans
are up to their ears in money that they don't know what
to do with. You say the long bond is stalled at 7^1/$_2$ percent? Not for long. When that money starts to pour into
New York, and it's only a matter of time before it does,
the rate will drop to 6 percent, maybe 5^1/$_2$ percent. Everybody, I mean everybody, has a vested interest in
lower interest rates. Right? And when rates fall, 3,000
on the Dow is a cinch."

Well, interest rates did *not* go down still further. In
fact, in the spring of 1987, they suddenly started to go

up. And this is where we arrived at Red Flag #1 where the stock market was concerned. Your broker was right: everybody, from the Treasury, to the Federal Reserve, to the banks, to corporate America, everybody *wanted* lower interest rates, because they would reinvigorate the economy and extend the already very long business recovery. However, a new parameter had been added to the situation, an international one, and one which suddenly had overriding importance: *our dependence on foreign capital.*

For we suddenly found ourselves in the position where we *had* to import $160 billion of foreign savings each year in order to fill the gap between the amount of money we needed to finance the $200 billion deficit (on top of all the capital needed by the private sector) and what we saved as a nation. Were the inflow of foreign savings to have abruptly stopped in spring 1987, it could have had disastrous financial and economic consequences. For the dollar was now beginning to weaken badly in foreign exchange markets around the world. And had foreigners become convinced in the spring of 1987 that the U.S. Government—the Treasury and the Federal Reserve—intended just to stand aside and let the dollar "find its own level," they would no doubt have chosen to stay away from any dollar investments. More specifically, the Japanese, who normally absorb as much as 40 percent of the new United States notes and bonds being sold each month to finance the budgetary deficit in Washington, might have chosen to stand aside completely. Were they to do so, bond prices would plummet, interest rates would skyrocket, and the financial outlook in the United States could suddenly darken to such a degree that these events could have led to an end of the recovery right there and then.

Paradoxically, the way to head off such an extreme situation was to tighten American monetary policy and *deliberately* raise interest rates above that $7\frac{1}{2}$ percent level which had prevailed for so long, the idea being to increase the *differential* between dollar and yen interest rates. If this differential was made large enough—i.e., pushed up to the $3\frac{1}{2}$ percent to 4 percent range where ten-year government notes were concerned—it would more than compensate for the prospect of further dollar devaluation over the life of these notes. When the Japanese ran the new numbers through their computers, and calculated how much more interest they would earn in dollars over ten years, as compared to what they would get if they stayed in yen, they would realize that this huge differential would protect them over the life of these notes even if the dollar sank to 120 yen to the dollar.

The new policy worked. The money kept coming in. But to keep it coming in, the yield on that thirty-year Treasury bond moved—*had* to move—from that 7.5 percent level (where it had been for over a year), first to 8 1/2 percent, then to 9 1/2 percent. Other key rates followed suit. The discount rate went from 5 1/2 percent to 6 percent. The prime rate went from 8 1/2 percent to 8 3/4 percent to 9 1/2 percent. Fixed thirty-year mortgages rose from 8 1/2 percent to well over 11 percent.

Then something strange started to happen. Despite this dramatic reversal in the direction of interest rates in the United States, the stock market kept going up. And up. And up. From the spring of 1987 to August 1987 the Dow moved 500 points higher. Now the linkage between what was happening in the credit market and the stock market had completely broken down. This was Red Flag #2.

Why did the market keep going up? Again, if you had called your stockbroker, he had a ready explanation.

"Forget interest rates. That was yesterday. Today it's a new ball game. Now the market is *profit*-oriented.

What's driving it up now are the huge, unprecedentedly huge, profits which America's great corporations are earning in 1987."

Unprecedentedly high corporate profits? Really?

Unfortunately not. To be sure, in 1987 corporate profits after taxes came in at $150 billion, way up from the previous year. But to put that number in perspective, in 1979, eight years earlier, they were $168 billion. In 1980 and 1981, when the Dow was in the 700's, they were higher than in 1987. So scratch the stockbroker's claim of "unprecedented corporate profits" as the reason why the stock market kept going up in the face of rapidly rising interest rates between the spring of 1987 and the fall.

If the wishful thinking inherent in this forecast had become apparent to you in the summer of last year, and you had sought a better explanation of what was happening, the answer this time would have been: "Forget 1987. It's going to be a good year. But it's *next* year's profits you must be looking at, and next year the sky's the limit. IBM will go to 250. GM to 125. The future never looked brighter."

I swear, I had lunch with one of this nation's biggest money managers at exactly this point in time, and that is exactly what he told me. And he was betting over $10 billion in the market on being right.

But was it not becoming increasingly apparent last summer that the great economic recovery which had begun in August 1982 was getting increasingly tired? That real growth was bound to slow in 1988? That if you combined slower growth with higher interest costs, profits were destined to peak in mid-1988? And that when recession became a reality a half year later, a decline—probably a precipitous decline—in corporate profitability would set in?

If you followed this logic, you had no choice but to also scratch *future* profits as the new driving force behind the soaring stock market.

Then what was driving the market to new high after new high now that neither the prospect of falling interest rates nor that of *sustainable* higher profits was realistic? My explanation is that between January and October 19 of 1987 the market was being propelled by what I term "the bandwagon effect." Meant here is that 85 percent of the trading on our stock exchanges was now done by institutions. The money that was being invested in the stock market during the first ten months of 1987 was coming principally from huge billion-dollar, even ten-billion-dollar pools of cash being accumulated by mutual funds, pension funds, insurance companies, trust departments of banks . . . money that used to go principally into bonds. But in 1987 bonds were for past generations. In this *new* investment age, the action, the only real action, was in the stock market. There, if you got smart guys to run your billions for you, 20 percent, even 30 percent, returns each year were a lead-pipe cinch. Right?

So even the most prudent of men, men responsible for tens upon tens of billions of *your* dollars, which you had entrusted to them in your pension fund, your mutual fund, your insurance company, increasingly turned to such "smart guys." Pension-fund managers, and others, began farming out an increasing proportion of their investable funds to them. And in order to squeeze out maximum "performance," these outside professionals were told that they would get paid strictly in accordance with how much they made. And on top of that, they were warned that each of them was in competition with the other outside money managers who were being brought in. If Tom was able to make only a 20 percent return, while Dick and Harry were making 30 percent plus, well . . .

So Tom, Dick, and Harry each get a billion from the pension fund of the public employees of the state of California, or that of the teachers in Texas, or from Aetna insurance company, and plow it straight into the stock market. In many cases, all of it. And sure enough, the more they put in, the more they earned. However, the poor guy among them who started to get scared as the market went from 2,000 to 2,500 to 2,700 and decided to play it safe—in bonds, or Treasury bills, or, God help us, cash—was left in the dust. And when, three months later, the results were toted up and compared, as bottom man, out he went. Back to the golf course in disgrace; replaced by a new Tom, but this time one who was more aggressive.

What this meant was that in a situation like this—and that was exactly the situation during the first ten months of 1987 when the bandwagon was rolling—nobody could afford to jump off, lest he end up as a money manager with no money to manage. Worse still, not only did he have to stay on the bandwagon, but he had to invest ever larger sums as the cash kept coming in. The watchword was, Be aggressive! You'll never see a market like this for the rest of your life!

Then, when the bandwagon came to a screeching halt

on October 19, 1987, everybody tried to jump off at once
—and the market plunged 508 points in six and a half
hours.

Reactions from Washington

What finally brought that bandwagon to a halt?

When you come right down to it, it was nothing more
than our old friend interest rates. The new Fed and
Treasury policy of keeping U.S. interest rates about $3\frac{1}{2}$
percent to 4 percent higher than those available in Japan or Europe, in order to keep foreign savings coming
in, worked perfectly well until Labor Day 1987. But
then a new element came into play: the domestic interest rates in Japan and Germany started to go up. The
yield on Japanese yen-denominated ten-year government notes, which only a year earlier had been $3\frac{1}{2}$ percent, now soared to over 6 percent, and in Germany
yields on DM-denominated government paper climbed
to almost 7 percent. That meant U.S. rates had to be
pushed into double digits. And in fact, on Monday, October 12, a week before the meltdown on Wall Street,

the yield on the long bond hit 10.44 percent. This was Red Flag #3, the reddest of red flags, one that signaled a serious threat of danger not just for the stock market, but for the entire economy. It had to be brought down quickly.

Secretary of the Treasury James A. Baker realized this, and hit the panic button. For he knew full well that if interest rates kept going up, if they had to keep going up in order to keep the foreign funds coming in, they would bring on a recession within six to nine months, i.e., before the presidential elections of November 1988. Yet if interest rates did *not* keep going up, the foreigners would start to balk, and the result might be even worse: an *involuntary*-interest-rate spike that would probably produce *instant* recession. Baker was between a rock and a hard place. Was there a way out?

There were, in fact, two:

- If Baker could convince Japan and Germany to loosen up their monetary and fiscal policies, and lower their interest rates immediately, this would allow the United States to do the same. Then the United States would have the best of both worlds: domestic interest rates could be lowered sufficiently to postpone the specter of recession beyond November 1988; and at the same time, if world interest rates went down in tandem, then that strategic 3 1/2 percent to 4 percent interest-rate differential in favor of the dollar could be maintained, and foreign savings would keep pouring in.

• The other course of action would involve engineering a sudden further devaluation of the dollar, making dollar investments, especially U.S. Government bonds, so much cheaper in terms of yen or DM that Japanese and European investors would continue to buy them *even if dollar interest rates were suddenly much lower, and the interest-rate differential was only 2 1/2 percent, not 3 1/2 percent.* Put another way, the "insurance premium" (in the form of the differential) demanded by foreign investors could be shrunk considerably if they became convinced that the new, lower international value of the dollar, after devaluation, was finally *sustainable.* U.S. interest rates could be cut by maybe two percentage points, yet foreign funds would nevertheless keep flooding our financial markets, and the economic situation could be saved.

Baker tried the first route at the beginning of that week, and decided to work on Germany first. The Germans came back with the suggestion that the Americans should first put their economic house in order before trying to boss the Germans. After all, who was Baker, a lawyer from Texas for God's sake, to tell the Herr Doktors with their degrees in economics from Heidelberg and Göttingen what to do?

Which really made Baker mad as hell. So he leaked a story to the New York *Times* saying that either the Germans play ball or he was going to drastically devalue the dollar against the mark. Then, he implied, we will see how many Mercedes and Volkswagens they'll still be able to sell in the United States. And when their unemployment rate rises from $8 1/2$ percent to $10 1/2$ percent as a result, we'll see who's smarter, Germans or Texans.

The *Times* ran it as their lead story on Sunday, October 18. And the financial world, the world of Wall Street, of the City of London, of the Bahnhofstrasse in Zurich, concluded that the Reagan administration had lost control. That America's economic destiny was no longer being run from Washington (where an obvious policy-making vacuum now existed) but was rather being dictated by Bonn and Tokyo. That the Americans were no longer masters of either their own interest rates or the value of the dollar in the foreign exchange markets. That, finally, Reaganomics was beginning to spell disaster.

And the next day the bottom fell out.

Unfortunately, the story does not end here. For, as I see it, this meltdown on Wall Street was just the precursor of the next, more serious crisis in our economic system. The initial drop, the first leg down into recession, will be just as precipitous as that first leg down into the bear market that happened on that Monday in October when a half trillion dollars of our national wealth disappeared in a frenzy of trading on our stock exchanges.

When will the next, much broader, crisis begin? In 1989, probably in February or March of 1989. But before the next one, the big one, occurs, we are being granted a period of grace . . . probably another nine months or so. But that will be all.

Looking Back

There are several lessons that must be heeded from the period that led up to October 19, 1987.

First, despite all my criticism of the phony euphoria that existed before the October 19 Panic—which was created in part by the professional money managers of this country—let's face it: you and I would have been damn fools not to go along with it at least part of the way and, if we were lucky, most of the way. All those hackneyed bits of advice like "Go with the flow" and "The trend is your friend" contain more than just a small portion of truth. The guys who cry "wolf" prematurely have often caused a lot of people to miss some very profitable financial boats. Prechter was *right* for most of 1987. Whether you attributed the market's rise from 2,000 to over 2,700 on the Dow in 1987 to a "fourth wave of optimism," as Prechter did, or to an irrational "bandwagon" effect, as I did in speech after speech last year, didn't matter a whit. If you had loaded up on stocks in the fall of 1986 and dumped them around Labor Day of 1987, you would have made the killing of your lifetime.

Sure, it's easy to say that *now*. But did anybody *really* call the October 19 Panic? In fact, was it "callable"?

No. Not a panic of *that* magnitude. Nobody in this universe thought that the New York stock market would ever go down 508 points in one trading session. Period.

But was the end of the Bull Market "predictable"?

Yes. I wrote the following in the October 1, 1987, issue of *Manhattan, inc.:* "The great bull market is essentially done for, done in by interest rates. Falling interest rates started this whole thing in the summer of 1982; rising interest rates in the fall of 1987 are going to kill it off."

In the final paragraph of that column I drew a comparison between the frenzied speculation in gold which had occurred a decade earlier and that which was occurring then in the stock market: "The Germans have a saying, *Die Bäume wachsen nicht in den Himmel.* Translation: 'The trees never grow into heaven.' The goldbugs —in the 1970's—found that out. The stock market bugs, who have succeeded them in the 1980's, are about to learn the same lesson."

Nineteen days later they did.

The head of the White House task force appointed to investigate the October Stock Market Panic, Nicholas F. Brady, an investment banker and former senator, summed up the reason why it happened with these words: "The stock market was incredibly high, by all standards that we measure it by." Simplistic. Yes. Essentially correct, absolutely . . .

The lesson to be learned: *Pay attention to those standards.* So,

1. If the average price-earnings ratios are 12 and 13 to 1, it is safe to buy.
2. When they reach 20 to 1, it is prudent to sell.
3. If yields on Blue Chip stocks are 4 percent, buy.
4. When they sink below 2 percent, sell.
5. When stocks sell for 1.25 times book value, buy.
6. When they sell for 2.5 times book, sell.

The most difficult decision, as most investment advisers know, is not when to buy, but when to sell. I followed my own advice and sold every stock I owned at the end of June 1987. Yes, I missed 200 points on the

Dow, but I got out way ahead . . . thank goodness. Next time around, I hope you remember these standards and get out too early rather than too late.

So much for the sermon of the day.

TWO

The Remaining Months Before the Crisis

THE WALL STREET JOURNAL CALLED THE DAY after October 19, 1987, "The most perilous day in 50 years."

In fact October 20 brought us right to the edge of seeing the Panic turn into a full-fledged nineteenth-century type of panic . . . one which, in turn, could have resulted in God only knows what kind of financial chaos, culminating in instant recession. We are lucky we still have a period of grace ahead of us before the next crisis hits; that we still have time to plan for the future where our money is concerned.

Just before the opening of the New York Stock Exchange on October 20, rumors started to fly that some of the key players in our financial system, the specialists on the floor of the New York Stock Exchange, faced imminent financial collapse. They had been caught in the middle, having loaded up on the shares they were "responsible for" all day Monday, only to see the prices completely fall out of sight in the final hour of trading. Two thirds of the specialists' total $3 billion in buying power had been wiped out. As a result, many specialists who had been hit hardest would begin the next day with their capital positions completely devastated.

At the opening on that Tuesday morning, it looked like salvation was in sight. The market opened up a never-seen 200 points, but the euphoria did not last long. A new wave of selling hit the floor of the exchange. By twelve-thirty the market was off 100 points, and looked like it had the potential to drop another 200 or 300. As the unfilled sell orders on such major stocks as IBM and Merck started to pile up, it looked like many of the floor specialists would have no option other than to fold. Having gotten hit two days in a row in an unprecedented fashion, some of them had simply run out of money. But the New York banks wouldn't lend them any more, and for good reason: their collateral—stocks, all of which were in free fall—was not acceptable. So trading ground to a halt.

The Wall Street Journal later described this moment in time as one when "the New York Stock Exchange died. But within an hour or two, it was raised from the dead."

Who raised it from the dead? The Federal Reserve Bank. At noon on Tuesday, October 20, it issued the following instructions to the major New York banks: "If anybody on Wall Street needs money quick, especially the specialists, lend it to them immediately. We will back you up with all the funding you might need."

The banks responded immediately, and as they began refinancing the specialists, the Federal Reserve began refinancing the banks. By one o'clock the specialists had regained enough financial confidence to begin executing orders once again. By two o'clock a major rally was under way. At the four o'clock closing the market was up a record 102.27 points in the Dow. The next day, as the liquidity kept pouring in, the market went up another 187 points. During the week M-1, the "hot" money in our system which is made up of cash and checking-account balances, skyrocketed by $10 billion. And by week's end, the crisis had passed, just as it had five years earlier when it was Mexico's lack of liquidity that threatened to bring the financial roof down on top of all of us.

Ironically, it was the need to rescue the tottering stock exchange that was at least partially responsible for the period of grace—between Panic and Crash—that we are still enjoying today. For as the Fed poured in the money, interest rates—those very high interest rates which had been threatening to bring an end to the recovery—plummeted by almost two full percentage points. The yield on the long bond—the thirty-year U.S. Government bond—dropped from just under 10.5 percent to just over 8.5 percent in a matter of days. It was not just the Fed that brought this about, however. A "flight to safety" had developed: vast amounts of money fled the stock market and moved into bonds, pushing prices up, yields down. In the subsequent weeks and months, interest rates stabilized, and ever since they have been held below levels which would be considered critical, allowing the economy to keep moving ahead during 1988, although as this year gets older, the pace of growth is beginning to slow. But you can be sure it won't stop before year's end.

Why? Because with not that many months to go now before the election, the cynic in me says that the Reagan administration will do everything in its power to keep interest rates as low as possible for the remainder of this year. If this requires a further jacking up of monetary growth and/or a further devaluation of the dollar—with potentially serious inflationary consequences further down the line—so be it. To be sure, we are told that the Federal Reserve Board acts independently. But no one can believe that it acts in a political vacuum, nor that its chairman is politically neutral. He's not. Alan Greenspan is a Republican. And he will act accordingly.

But an economy cannot survive on monetary policy alone. After a certain point, pushing more money into the system increasingly resembles pushing on a string. For in the end, just as with the stock market, it is the *real* factors that will dictate the shape of things to come.

And when you look at the real economy in this year 1988, you *must* conclude that it is very, very close to running out of steam. Because the only remaining *oomph* in the system is coming from consumer spending.

If you look at the other three traditional sources of economic stimulus—capital spending, government spending, and international trade—you will realize why the time has come to get worried. All three have already stalled. When consumer spending stops growing, that stall will turn into a dive. And we are off and falling into recession.

Capital Spending

Capital spending, dollar for dollar the most potent force in our economy, is today a spent force. It always tails off near the end of a business recovery. But now, with equity capital very difficult to raise in the aftermath of Black Monday, and very expensive if you can get it, and with concern growing about the nation's immediate economic future, nobody in his right corporate mind is about to embark upon a major expansion of production facilities. In fact, like Chrysler, they are doing precisely the opposite. The gradual increase in layoffs and plant closings that you are seeing right now is the best indication of what corporate America expects in the near future: too much output capacity, not too little. So scratch capital spending.

Government Spending

Then what about government spending? After all, the impetus for growth provided by government spending has been the key to the great recovery of the 1980's, one that we are still enjoying. Boring as it may be to talk yet again about the deficits in Washington, the fact of the matter is that without them who knows where we would be today, especially in terms of unemployment. The reason why the United States is near full employment right now goes directly back to those $200 billion plus deficits that were run, year after year, by Ronald Reagan. They provided a Keynesian type of economic stimulus on a scale that could only be imagined a decade ago.

What does that mean—"Keynesian stimulus"? How does it work? And what happens when it is overdone, exhausting its efficacy? These are questions that should have been sharply debated in Washington over the past six years, but have been largely ignored.

The concept has its origins in the teachings of John Maynard Keynes, the most brilliant economist of this century, yet one of the most maligned—and maligned by, of all people, Ronald Reagan. Reagan, when he took office, had us believe that what he was about to do represented something new in the field of economics—called Reaganomics. In actual fact, when you look back, it was Keynesian economics applied in spades: the President created prosperity through artificial stimulation of demand by running unprecedentedly large governmental deficits.

The idea of using governmental deficits to promote economic growth had its origins in the economic chaos of the 1930's. The theory that had prevailed before the decade of the Great Depression was that government intervention in the economy designed to generate demand, and, ultimately, employment, was not necessary: that supply creates its *own* demand. This became known as Say's Law, after the French economist, Jean Baptiste Say, who first "discovered" it, and it was soon considered an immutable law, one that was as eternally valid as the law that explained why Newton's apple fell from the tree.

And it was logical. You made something, like a buggy whip, you got paid for it, and then you used that money to buy something of equivalent value, a peck of potatoes. Supply created its own demand. Right? So there was no reason that the population as a whole must ever be underemployed because of insufficient demand for the goods and services they were capable of producing.

The problem was that this "law" seemed to be suspended with great regularity. Throughout the nineteenth century there were constantly recurring economic crises—panics and crashes, followed by recessions and high unemployment—caused, it would seem, by an "oversupply." To be sure, these interludes never lasted very long. Usually within a matter of less than a year such oversupply would disappear as the people who had lost their jobs in bankrupt buggy whip companies found jobs in new enterprises producing new products, like spark plugs. With their incomes back on stream, as they once again got paid for contributing to the new "supply" of products, they would start buying again. This renewed demand would sop up the oversupply that had been hanging over the market and, within a very short time, order, balance, and equilibrium were restored, meaning employment for anybody who wanted to work. After all, according to Say's Law, "Supply always creates its own demand."

All this made sense, more or less, until the Great

Crash—the Crash of '29, after which a situation developed that had no precedent. An oversupply of unprecedented proportions developed, with the result that tens of thousands of factories stopped production, ten thousand banks closed their doors and never reopened, and farmers throughout the country burned their crops and abandoned their land. The Depression was not just an American phenomenon: the economies of Britain, Germany, France, Italy, even Switzerland were similarly devastated and the entire world was adversely affected in the 1930's.

In the midst of all this misery rose the voice of the Cambridge economist John Maynard Keynes. He said that Say had been dead wrong, that classical nineteenth-century economics was all wet. All one had to do was look around. By 1936, 20 percent of the industrialized world's labor force was out of work. The only explanation for this was that supply quite obviously did *not* create an equal amount of demand. Just because somebody made something did not mean that somebody else would buy it. Equilibrium did *not* return to the system if it got sufficiently out of whack. Mass employment would not necessarily go away if we simply relied on "the system," the "invisible hand" of Adam Smith, to do so. Because, Keynes pointed out, the system had broken down. There simply was not enough *demand* to create jobs for everybody who wanted to work. The result was a shortfall of jobs of such magnitude that the very social fabric of the capitalistic world was at stake.

If the problem was inadequate *demand*, and if the "supply side" did not itself produce such demand, what were we to do about it?

Artificially stimulate demand, said Keynes. But who could do this, and how could it be done? The answer to the "who" was government; the answer to the "how" was deficit spending. If governments followed his advice, they would begin to spend more money than they took in, borrow the difference, and distribute the money by one means or another to the people so that they could, in effect, buy themselves out of the Depression.

But Keynes's prescription for economic policy did not end there. The theory which he expounded also postulated that when the economy eventually recovered, tax receipts would soar to such levels that governments could easily repay what they had borrowed to set things in motion again. The idea, then, was remarkably simple: governments should run deficits to thwart recession, but, once the downturn was overcome, should run surpluses during the ensuing times of prosperity, building up a reservoir of reserve stimulus, ready for possible deployment during the next downturn in the business cycle.

The Reagan administration got the first part right, from 1982 to 1985, but failed miserably on the follow-through in subsequent years. And that, in a sentence, is basically why we are facing such a mess in 1989.

Reagan inherited a highly dangerous inflationary situation from Jimmy Carter (and inflation can destroy the fabric of society just as easily as unemployment). As we have noted, Paul Volcker defused that situation by tightening money and credit to such a degree that the nation plunged into a sharp "inflation cleansing" recession in 1981. In August 1982, in response to the Mexican debt crisis, the monetary brakes were taken off, and the way was opened for economic recovery thereafter. All that was needed was fiscal stimulus. The Reagan administration followed the Keynesian prescription for such a situation almost to the letter: it started to run huge deficits. The economy took off like a big bird, and kept rising in 1983, 1984, 1985.

But so did the deficits keep rising. Much lower tax

rates combined with a much-lower-than-expected tax base (because of the plummeting rates of inflation) resulted in much-lower-than-expected tax receipts. On the other side of the ledger, in my opinion, huge but necessary increases in the defense budget, combined with runaway entitlement like Medicare and Medicaid programs, resulted in much higher expenditures than originally anticipated. The result: a deficit that was getting out of control.

This was the point, the year 1985, at which Reagan should have reversed course and increased taxes, especially indirect taxes (such as gasoline, cigarette, and alcohol taxes which do not destroy entrepreneurial incentives) sufficiently to correct the situation before it got totally out of hand. He didn't. The moment passed. The band played on. The government kept on artificially stimulating consumer demand by running *still* higher deficits when the economy was already going full blast. The process finally reached the point where there was now so *much* demand, excess demand, in the system that it started to spill abroad, chasing goods made in Japan and Hong Kong and Stuttgart. This was Keynesian economics gone haywire.

Somebody should have tried to explain this to Reagan

and pointed out to him that all of his immediate prede-
cessors had been doing the same thing—that the United
States had been running deficits for twenty-four out of
twenty-five years—that the Keynesian medicine had
continued to work and work well, for Democrat and
Republican alike. The difference was that in the past the
demand stimulation by government had been moderate,
and had been typified by a pattern of ebb and flow.
Since 1981 it has been all flow. And the flow has reached
such proportions that the medicine no longer works.
The runaway Reagan deficits have driven the national
debt from under $1 trillion to well over $2 trillion. As a
result, the government's borrowing needs have been
greatly outpacing domestic savings. The gap just had to
be filled somehow, and it was done in a new way, by our
importation of vast amounts of foreign savings. The
United States suddenly was on the road to accumulating the world's largest international debt—maybe $1
trillion dollars by decade's end—which would ultimately make our nation hostage to our creditors in Japan and Europe.

The realization that this was the road to ruin finally
produced a reaction in Washington, but it came from

Congress, not the White House. And its form was the Gramm-Rudman-Hollings Act which mandated the first deficit reduction in the 1980's by way of automatic across-the-board cuts, a so-called "no-brainer" solution. The process worked in fiscal year 1987, and the deficit plunged from well over $200 billion to under $150 billion. Gramm-Rudman II would have dictated another $25 billion in cuts had Congress not volunteered cuts of at least that much on their own. It did to the magnificent tune of $30 billion. Cynics would point out this was much too little, much too late.

For the point of the rather long dissertation on Keynesian economics you just suffered through is this: we no longer have the ace of deficit spending in the hole. Reagan and the Congress have so misused their power to run deficits that their efficacy has been lost. Just when we could use the dynamics of deficit spending to counter the threat of recession in 1989, we are precluded from employing it. For our situation is so precarious that even the hint of higher deficits could lead to a total collapse in the international value of the dollar, and worldwide monetary and economic chaos.

I can only conclude that where fiscal policy is concerned the government is essentially powerless in re-

gard to preventing a recession in 1989, no matter what
happens in 1989.

International Trade and the "J" Curve

The third sector of the economy, the international one,
at one time seemed to represent possible salvation. It
was hoped that with the tremendous devaluation of the
dollar—50 percent since the beginning of 1985 against
the other key international currencies—imports would
collapse and exports increase significantly. The theory
was that as this happened, the trade deficit would decline from $165 billion in 1986 to $135 billion in 1987 to
well under $100 billion this year.

The turnaround would begin with a sudden decline
in imports which would result in a massive repatriation
of American purchasing power. Tens upon tens of billions of dollars of American demand would no longer
be directed toward Hondas, would no longer be stimulating so much output and employment in Japan, but
would return to Detroit, to Fords and Cadillacs, and
promote output and employment in the United States.
Theoretically, this process could have more than fully

compensated for the withdrawal of demand stimulus from the governmental sector under Gramm-Rudman, and extended this recovery into 1990, and maybe beyond.

But, alas, it has not worked out that way. In fact, in 1987 as the dollar kept sinking, the trade deficit kept getting larger, culminating in monthly deficits in the second half of last year in the range of $15 billion to $17 billion a month, which, if continued unabated, would soon add up to $200 billion a year! What happened? The standard explanation for this is the "J" curve . . . a shorthand way of saying that a nation's foreign trade situation always gets worse following a currency devaluation (the left-hand side of the "J"), then it bottoms out (the middle), and finally begins to improve rapidly (the right-hand side): thus the "J."

Why this sequence of events? Especially, why did things have to get worse before they get better as a result of the massive dollar devaluation which began in 1985? Because as the dollar's value sank, making imported goods more expensive, it took a while before we Americans began shying away from imports because of their now higher prices. Our buying habits change slowly, and if one of our beloved Yuppies was hell-bent on buying a Porsche to prove what a hotshot he is, a price increase of 10 percent or 20 percent would hardly deter him, at least while the good times were still rolling on Wall Street.

In addition, the delay between devaluation and an improvement in our trade deficit was made even longer due to the fact that for several months, despite a continuing fall in the value of the dollar abroad, in many cases the price of imported products did not change one iota. For although the producers of that Yuppie-bound Porsche back in Deutschland were getting less and less DM for each car they shipped to the United States (when a car was sold for $50,000 in 1985 the German manufacturer received DM 100,000, since the exchange rate was 2.00 DM to the dollar, but he only got DM 90,000 in 1986 when the dollar was only worth DM 1.80), the Stuttgart-based company only increased its dollar prices reluctantly. Porsche simply could not stand to lose market share in the United States to Jaguar or the new high-performance Japanese models which were now hitting the American market. And Porsche could afford this since the profit margins on the cars they had sold to Americans prior to the onset of dollar devaluation were nothing short of obscene.

However, when the exchange rate continued to sink toward DM 1.70 to the dollar, even Porsche's profit margins began to completely disappear, and, whether it affected market share or not, Porsche was finally forced to start raising the dollar price of each unit. For a while most American consumers, like our Yuppie two paragraphs above, didn't seem to care. They kept buying the same number of Porsches as before, even though the price had now started to rise rapidly. The same phenomenon happened where Mercedes, Toyotas, Rolexes, and Sony televisions were concerned. Result: the value of imports actually kept *rising* following devaluation. This was what one economist terms "the necessary valley of fire through which we had to pass to go to the other side."

As a result of the most recent moves in the value of the dollar, it would seem that we have finally arrived on the other side. A sign that we are now on the right side of that "J" curve is what has recently happened to the Porsche automobile company back in Deutschland. American demand for their cars suddenly dropped to such a degree that the company is now forced to shut down its assembly line periodically. This year Porsche has had to cut way back on its labor force in Stuttgart.

They also fired the man in charge of sales in the United States, and replaced him with a German. As if that will help. It would seem that, finally, Secretary of the Treasury Baker, and not the Herr Doktors from Heidelberg, is having the last word. For gradually the sales of Rolexes and French wines and Swiss chocolates are now also declining. At the same time European unemployment is rising.

The situation in 1988 is being helped by another factor—an extraneous factor over which we really have no control—namely, the cost of oil. Crude oil is by far the largest single item where imports are concerned, amounting to around $45 billion last year, or more than one quarter of our entire trade deficit. Last year the average price of that oil was around $20 a barrel; this year it will be 20 percent to 25 percent less. That, alone, will reduce our imports by $10 billion.

Factor in what is happening to our exports, and the foreign trade picture is beginning to look still better. For our exports are now also starting to respond to the fact that the massive dollar devaluation has made American products much cheaper throughout most of the world.

However, when you add it all up, the help that is

beginning to come from international trade in 1988 is a classic example of too little, too late. Even if the swing in our trade situation had been more dramatic, in the greater scheme of things it still would have not made that much difference. For this sector represents only 15 percent of our total economy. The percentage pales in significance when you compare it to the importance of the American consumers' economic power: they control 68 percent of all the spending in our economic system. If *their* demand suddenly begins to fall off, then all of us will be in trouble.

Unfortunately, that is precisely what is going to happen, and probably within less than a year.

Consumer Spending

Why? Because growth in consumer spending at the present time relates directly to increases in consumer debt: we are living beyond our means, and we are able to do so only by accumulating ever higher debts. The problem is that this process of debt accumulation is doomed to end soon since our debt burden is approaching intolerable levels. In 1988 the *financial charges facing the average American family will exceed 50 percent of its take-home pay: half* of what comes in goes immediately out for the mortgage, for payments on the car, for last year's vacation, for payments on the different credit cards we all use. Many economists believe that this 50 percent represents the ceiling, even if all other factors affecting the cost of *servicing* this massive consumer debt remained equal. But they are not equal.

Interest rates are a full 2 percent higher than a year ago. And, increasingly, interest costs are no longer fully deductible expenses where taxes are concerned. Only mortgage interest remains eligible. The combination of these three factors—the level of debt, higher interest costs on that debt, and the loss of interest-cost deductibility—is a deadly one. Meaning that the carrying cost of past consumer excesses finally becomes unbearable. By the end of this year growth in consumer spending in the United States will stop.

And the whole American economy, with no major force left to propel it forward any longer, will stall, and then begin to slide back. The first to go will be new construction of plant and equipment as manufacturers anticipate cutbacks in consumer spending; then housing starts will plummet; automobile sales will start to recede, then those of appliances. The downward spiral accelerates as the loss of demand for these end products works its way back through the pipeline—lumber sales will slump, so will those of steel and aluminum and electronic components. And then the layoffs will begin in earnest in the lumber mills in Oregon and car assembly plants in Michigan and, yes, even in Silicon Valley in California; and as incomes disappear, demand will start to fall in earnest. The downward spiral will begin to perpetuate itself. As the consumption of energy starts to drop, pushing oil prices down even further, the incomes of those states so dependent on the petroleum industry—Texas, Oklahoma, Colorado, Louisiana—will literally plummet, making things still worse. We have arrived at a new case of "oversupply" and we are at the beginning of the Recession of '89.

We have also arrived at one of the most critical issues to be addressed in this book: what will be the shape of this recession in 1989? Will it be fairly long and deep and be shaped like a "V"? Or will it be shallow and longer and resemble a "U"? Or will it, as some suggest, go totally out of control, meaning that in the end we will end up in The Great Depression of the 1990's?

Investment Strategy for 1988

But before addressing those questions, let's pause for a moment and consider how we should be planning for the Recession of '89 in terms of our personal finances. What we are talking about is not just adjusting your portfolio with your broker, but shifting your holdings in your IRA, Keogh plan, 401K savings plan, or mutual funds.

Stocks

Here we are faced with three alternatives: To buy, to sell, or to do neither—to just put our stock market activities on hold and ride it out.

About the last thing I would do right now is buy stocks. Because in my opinion, during the next twelve months stocks are bound to get a lot cheaper than they are now. When the investing public (and the money managers) finally are forced to face the inevitability of recession in '89, they are going to be forced to come up with the answers to some very basic questions.

There are three key points that every investor must consider:

1. When recession hits the economy next year, what's going to happen to the earnings of IBM and General Motors and Merck and Kodak? They are going to go down.

2. As the mood of the country, and the world, turns negative, what kind of multiple will the market put on these much lower earnings? Are we looking at price-earnings ratios of 20 to 1, 15 to 1, or 10 to 1? Probably 10 to 1. That would probably put the Dow at 1,200 or lower.

3. What would that do to yields? Put them back up to the 4 percent plus level. And at these much lower price levels, stocks would once again be selling at 150 percent of book value.

My conclusion, faced with this outlook, is that a year from now will be the time to buy stocks, not now.

All right, but what to do about the stocks and the mutual funds you still own? Should you dump them? After all, if the market's going lower, why hang on? Frankly, if I still owned any stocks, which I don't, I would sell, and sell right now. I am not saying that we are necessarily on the brink of Black Monday II. What I am saying is that we are most probably going to see a steady erosion in stock prices in the months ahead, for the reasons given above. So why just sit there and be nickeled and dimed to death?

But most people are not like me. I watch the market every day. To me a sell decision is as easy to arrive at as a buy decision. But most people are not like that. They simply do not have the time or the inclination to "play" the ups and downs of the market.

If you find yourself in this profile, what's the best move for you? You might be best advised just to ride this one through, and not get too clever with going in and out of the market, paying a lot of commissions, and risking getting whipsawed in the process.

Well, the answer to that one depends on two things:

- How long will stocks remain depressed?

- And what will the other side of the Recession of '89 look like?

The answer to both of these questions could speak in favor of "riding it out." Because, in my judgment, the next recession is not going to be a long, dragged-out affair. It is going to resemble a "V" not a "U." It will definitely not turn into a depression. Secondly, I think you might be surprised at how optimistic I am about the 1990's where our economy is concerned. If you wait it out, you will probably find yourself in a much healthier and more stable world in the early 1990's, a world in which 3,000 on the Dow will be justified.

So, for those of you who are willing to hang on, to suffer some major "paper" losses in your holdings next year, my recommendation is to hold on to your mutual funds as well as your individual stocks.

Bonds

Bonds are an unequivocal *buy*. Why? Because long-term interest rates are about to peak out. We are in the final stage of the business recovery that started way back in the fall of 1982, one that is about to end for the reasons given earlier in this chapter. The ideal time to buy bonds is always right before the onset of a recession. Why? Because in the ultimate stages of a period of extended prosperity, exactly where we are now, the demand for credit reaches a final crescendo, meaning that interest rates do the same.

Therefore now is the time to begin locking in these prerecession high interest rates before they take a dive next year. My advice is to buy when long-term yields reach 9 1/2 percent, not before.

Why will interest rates dive in the first half of '89? Because they are going to be pulled down by the absence of demand for credit and the absence of inflation. And then the value of the bonds you buy now will go up, probably up by quite a bit: 25 percent at least.

What kind of bonds should you buy? The safest. Stick to U.S. Government bonds. How should you buy them? Probably the best way is to buy into a no-load government bond fund, one that concentrates on bonds with long maturities. The Benham Group, based in Palo Alto, California, has a whole string of such funds under its management and is probably the best place to go.

How much should you invest in bonds? I would say as much as half of the funds you currently have available for investment purposes. How long should you plan on keeping them? For one year. Then sell. Because when the crisis hits in mid-1989, interest rates are going to skyrocket . . . at least temporarily. But more of that in Chapter 4.

One final piece of advice: stay away from junk bonds. How do you tell what a junk bond is? By its excessively high yield. Any time a bond salesman calls you up and offers you bonds paying 12 percent plus, hang up the phone. Because the companies that issue these junk bonds are headed for big trouble. And if you own some of their paper, you might end up holding a big bagful of nothing.

Gold and Silver

Not yet. With inflation about to collapse as a result of the onset of recession in '89, inflation hedges such as precious metals are not going to go anywhere in the immediate future. But a year from now that will change. When *fear* will take over.

So wait.

Real Estate

When recession hits, foreclosures are going to mount rapidly. Savings and loans are then going to have to dump a lot of properties in order to stay liquid, to stay open. That will depress the entire real estate market in 1989. So if you like real estate as an investment, and I very definitely do, stay liquid.

CDs, T-bills, Money Market Accounts

I would keep at least half of my money in any one of these (if you can't get a $9^1/2$ percent yield in bonds, consider putting all your money here). In other words, put half of your investable funds in government bonds and keep the other half in these short-term investments. Your principal is completely safe where T-bills are concerned; it is equally safe if you restrict your investment in bank CDs and money market accounts to $100,000 per bank. Your income on the money is decent—the interest you get is well above the rate of inflation, keeping you ahead of the game in terms of purchasing power. Provided you stick to three-month maturities where your T-bills and CDs are concerned, you will be totally liquid if some emergency hits you during the coming recession. And when some bargains crop up as a result of that recession, you will have cash during a time when cash will be king.

Defensive Strategy

In economic times like these, you need to consider not just how to make money, but, more importantly, how to protect the assets you already have.

When bad times come, the people who get hurt first and get hurt the most are those who are overindebted. The danger is that, though we might be okay today where our debt-to-income situation is concerned, we might get blindsided tomorrow by a sudden surge in interest rates. This brings us directly to your mortgage, because for most of us this is *the* big debt in our life. For those of you who have a thirty-year fixed-rate mortgage there is obviously nothing to worry about. The problem is that an increasing number of us now have *adjustable*-rate mortgages, and our monthly payments can vary drastically depending on what interest rates in general do in the future. That 7½ percent rate you started with (and this low starting rate is probably what prompted you to go the "adjustable route") can jump to 12½ percent very quickly, and suddenly your house payments will be $7,000 or $8,000 a year higher than you budgeted for, perhaps higher than you will be able to afford.

But what are the odds on that happening next year? Don't interest rates usually go *down* not up in a recession. Yes. And that is precisely what I think is going to happen in the *initial* phases of the Recession of '89, I stress, *in the initial phases.* And I think they will probably go way down. But they might not stay down for very long. In fact, the odds are at least 50 percent that within six months of the plunge, they might, I stress *might,* begin to rise again, perhaps quite rapidly and quite substantially, and end up at much higher levels than those prevailing today. That they *might* force your mortgage rate right up to the "cap" in your mortgage agreement, which is normally at a level five percentage points higher than where you are right now. Are you prepared for this eventuality?

If not, why run the risk of getting financially whipsawed by such an interest-rate roller coaster which may be part of our immediate future? My suggestion: if you are in the market for a new mortgage or if you already have an adjustable-rate mortgage, obtain, or convert to, a new type of mortgage which may well allow you to have your cake and eat it, too. I'm referring to a fixed/

adjustable hybrid, namely, *a variable-rate mortgage that is fixed for the first five years.* That will take you through the "roller coaster interest-rate stage" which might lie ahead. You can lock in a rate of less than 10 percent for the initial five-year "fixed" phase. And when that five years is up in 1993, if my forecasts work out, we will probably arrive at a new era in which interest rates will be both lower and more stable than they are today. You will have enjoyed the best of both worlds.

Now let me suggest something else in the nature of "defensive debt strategy" which, at first, will probably seem contradictory. Take some time out and go to the trouble of obtaining a backup credit facility from your bank. Get as large a *line*—$50,000 to $100,000 (you don't have to use it, nor do you want to use it)—of *unsecured* credit as you can. Get it while the good times are still here, when your income is still high, when the value of your assets is unimpaired. In other words, get it now while the getting is still good.

You never know, when people start to get laid off next year, one of your family might be among them. And another might get sick. You know how it goes at times. You might suddenly be faced with an urgent need for cash and it would come at a time when the economy is depressed, during a period when the banks are very reluctant to take on new loan commitments, when you could take a fierce financial licking if you had to revert to selling some of your assets, even your home, in order to raise cash.

The unsecured credit line that you were smart enough to set up in the summer of 1988 may end up saving the day in 1989. And the day would be saved. You could draw down $50,000. The crisis would be bridged. The recession would end. Everybody would be back at work again. You would pay back the loan. And you would come out on the other side with your assets, especially your home, intact.

A lot of people who have not planned for the worst will not be as lucky. For 1989 is going to be a very difficult year.

1989

The Crisis

Three

The Crisis

WHAT HAPPENED ON MONDAY, OCTOBER 19, 1987, is definitely a predictor of worse things to come in our economy. Is this thesis, one that postulates that an economic downturn is more or less inevitable after a major market plunge, historically valid? Have stock market crashes almost always been followed by recession or depression in modern times?

The answer is definitely yes. Consider the record since the beginning of this century:

MARKET DOWNTURN	PERCENTAGE DECLINE IN DOW JONES AVERAGE
Market downturn began January 19, 1906 Economic slump began in May 1907	48.5
Market downturn began November 21, 1916 Economic slump began in August 1918	40.1
Market downturn began November 3, 1919 Economic slump began in January 1920	46.6
Market downturn began September 3, 1929 The Great Depression began a year later	89.2
Market downturn began March 10, 1937 The nation fell back into Depression in May 1937	49.1
Market downturn began November 12, 1938 World War Two began eleven months later and no slump developed	41.3
Market downturn began December 3, 1968 Economic slump began December 1969	35.9
Market downturn began January 11, 1973 Economic slump began November 1973	45.1
Market downturn began August 25, 1987 Economic slump *predicted* to begin February 1989	36.1

Basing my opinion on these historical precedents alone, if we did *not* have a recession, it would represent a highly unusual aberration.

But why the long "lag" of fifteen months between October 19, 1987, and my suggested starting date of February/March 1989 as the starting date for the next recession? Historically, the "grace period" has been somewhat shorter.

The principal reason is that interest rates fell dramatically following the October 19 Panic because, as we have noted, the Federal Reserve flooded the New York money market with liquidity in the week that followed. Since then there has been a continuing flight to safety as large numbers of American investors have been opting for U.S. Government bonds rather than stocks, pushing the prices of those bonds higher and keeping long-term interest rates in general one percentage point lower than they were pre-Crash. The economy, aided by the fact that long-term rates have remained in single digits, is therefore continuing to move forward somewhat longer than one would normally expect after a market crash.

Second, as we have noted, because of the massive devaluation of the dollar, which continued after Black

Monday (and as far as I know, the phenomenon of *simultaneous* crashes in both the stock market and the dollar is unique in this century), we are seeing a turnaround in our foreign trade position—more exports and an increasing amount of import substitution. Both mean higher domestic output in 1988 than would have occurred in the absence of devaluation.

But as we have also noted, the dominant force in our economy—consumer buying—is just about spent, and when it begins to weaken, the negative impact will overwhelm the remaining positive forces in our system and result in the onset of recession in early 1989.

Now to a major point. I am of the opinion that the market plunge of October 19, 1987, is not just a predictor of an economic downturn in terms of *time*, i.e., that recession will begin with a lag of a year, give or take a few months, as it almost always has historically. I am *further* suggesting that what happened on Black Monday is a precursor of the course the next recession will follow, at least in its initial phases. More specifically, I feel that just as the market dropped an unprecedented 23 percent in one day, a downturn so precipitous that it is without historical precedent, *so also will the first step down into recession in 1989 be precipitous.*

Leaving the stock market as a predictor aside, are there other reasons, are there *economic* grounds, for such a prediction? There are, and they are of both a national and an international nature.

The Leveraging of Corporate America

Starting at home, once recession begins, the odds are now very high that it will set off a cascade of major corporate bankruptcies in the United States. As the cascade develops, medium- and small-sized firms—suppliers of the major companies—will be sucked into the vortex, and we will soon see a disruption of corporate America's output—and the income it produces for all of us—of an unusual magnitude. This process will trigger a plunge in overall activity of the entire American economy of an unusual nature.

The man who originally came up with this thesis, in a speech in San Francisco last year, was, of all people, William Seidman, the chairman of the Federal Deposit Insurance Corporation, the agency which insures all of our bank deposits up to $100,000. Normally a man in this key position considers himself duty-bound to spread cheer at all times, to exude unlimited confidence. Not Mr. Seidman, to his eternal credit.

What has prompted him to go on the public record with such worries? His recognition of the highly dangerous *overleveraging* of corporate America that exists today. This is the same factor that, according to John J. Phelan, Jr., chairman of the New York Stock Exchange, was one of the primary reasons behind the crash on Wall Street. "Everybody has been aware of the concern about the 'leveraging' of America, and the markets," he said to the New York *Times*. "Leverage works terrific going up, but terrible going down."

Exactly. And where the leveraging of corporate America has gone way beyond tolerable limits is in the explosion of leveraged buyouts (LBOs) financed by the issue of junk bonds. At least one hundred major American corporations have gone this route.

The phenomenon of LBOs stems from an all-American mixture of greed and ego. It usually starts with greed, the greed that motivates corporate raiders out to make a quick buck. These are often not so nice guys who spot a company which, they figure, is way undervalued in the stock market, especially if you approach "value" by examining a company's assets. Their method of operation is to buy up all the company's stock "on the cheap" through a tender offer, and then to gradually break up the corporation by selling it off, one division after the other in separate transactions, adding the proceeds to the cash hoard the company had already built up before the raider attacked it, and then liquidate the shell corporation that is left over. At the end of the process—which maybe will take only a couple of years —the raider ends up getting, say, $2 billion out of a company he paid only $1 billion for in the first place. The British invented this sort of thing decades ago. They call the people who do it "asset strippers." They are not the most beloved among men there either.

Often they do not succeed, since they bump into another formidable force, ego. The ego belongs to the CEO of the company that the asset stripper is trying to raid, and then rape. That CEO, faced with a hostile takeover of *his* baby, the one he has spent twenty of the best years of his life building into the $1 billion corporation it is today, comes to the conclusion that he has no choice but to fight back. If the outside raider is successful, he will lose not only his baby, but also the corporate Learjet, the company's apartment in London's West End, the corporate rest and recreation facility in the

Bahamas—all of which he really considers *his* personal perks, since it was, after all, *he* who built the company to what it is today. So the CEO decides that he is duty-obligated to snatch the company from the greedy raider by buying it himself. However, in contrast to the asset stripper, he does not want to break it up. He just wants to remain a Big Man, to be invited next year to the summer encampment of the Bohemian Club and be able to piss on the same redwood tree that Henry Kissinger and Walter Wriston use.

The problem is that he, and the senior management of the company, whom he usually brings into the deal, do not have all that much money. Enter the LBO. They pool their limited amount of capital and then "leverage" it tremendously by borrowing ten times as much as they put up. They proceed to make the public share-holders an offer they can't refuse; i.e., they offer to pay a price appreciably higher than that being offered by the raider, and if it all works out, they end up owning the company.

But they also end up way over their heads financially. If, on a billion-dollar buyout, the members of our management team can scrape together only $100 million of their own money and are forced to borrow the rest—$900 million—they end up facing absolutely staggering financial charges, especially if the company had a lot of debt to begin with. Interest rates on the huge loans can vary from 12 to 18 percent and the front-end fees to the people who arrange them are enormous: they resemble "points" that your greedy bank charges at the front end when it gives you a mortgage.

In a transaction like this, everything will work out *provided* the economy remains prosperous and their company keeps doing well. The theory behind leveraged buyouts is that they will be financed by retained earnings and internally generated cash flow. The problem is that many of these corporations are barely able to make their payments now, during times of still-high prosperity. What, you should ask, is going to happen to their earnings and cash flow, and thus their ability to meet their financial obligations, when the crisis hits at the beginning of 1989?

To exemplify the type of accident that is just waiting to happen, take Safeway Stores, one of the largest food retailers in the world. Safeway was being run perfectly well by Peter Magowan, the Oxford-educated grandson of the founder. Then along came the raiders in the form of the dreaded Haft family of Washington, D.C.—Dart

Drug Stores and Crown Books—with a hostile takeover bid. Magowan, refusing to even entertain the thought of working for the Hafts, went the LBO route, borrowing $4.3 billion at between 12 and 15 percent to finance the rescue. Safeway already owed $1.1 billion. Net result: annual financial charges paid by the company exceeded $500 million. Safeway earnings were $231 million. Which left a slight gap. So how was the gap filled? By selling off assets on a massive scale: in other words, doing exactly what the management buyout of the company was supposedly designed to *prevent*. First it was Safeway, U.K., that was sold. Then the stores in Utah and around Dallas and El Paso. Then the entire Liquor Barn subsidiary. Then all the stores in the Midwest. Then Safeway, Australia. Then all the stores in Southern California. All in all, just under one thousand stores have been spun off, reducing the size of Safeway from a pre-LBO total of 2,392 stores to only 1,399 at present. What this means is that Safeway is meeting today's enormous cash-flow needs by selling assets that should represent tomorrow's earnings. What happens when tomorrow arrives in the form of recession? Reach your own conclusion.

If we are looking for worse examples, there are plenty

around. Southland Corporation, the company that controls the 7-Eleven chain of convenience stores, was bought back from the public by the three sons of the founder through a leveraged buyout. To swing the deal, they borrowed $2.5 billion in the first stage at an average interest rate of 18 percent. As part of the second-stage financing, they were going to issue junk bonds that would accumulate interest at this rate, but it would not be paid out. Instead, after three to five years, they would issue new junk bonds in lieu of the accumulated but not paid interest, and these new bonds would be of the same type. Can you believe it? At the end of the road, when faced with the balloon payment to end all balloon payments, how in the world will the debtors be able to meet their obligations—even in good times?

Then there are the corporations that are making themselves unattractive to raiders by taking on enormous new debt and immediately paying out the proceeds in the form of a one-time cash dividend to shareholders. One used to accuse American corporations of planned obsolescence. Now one can justly accuse them of planned corporate suicide.

The fault for introducing this highly dangerous corporate overleveraging into our economy—highly dangerous for all of *us* ultimately—by no means rests exclusively with asset strippers and/or egocentric CEOs of our corporations. Everybody, it seems, was out to make a killing through the junk-bonding of America. The investment bankers, whose traditional role was that of *building* America by raising capital for the construction of our railroads in the nineteenth century, our high-tech industries in the twentieth, have been falling all over themselves trying to make a quick buck setting corporations up for *destruction* in the form of liquidation if everything works out, or Chapter 11 if it doesn't. On the Beatrice deal alone they charged fees amounting to a quarter of a *billion* dollars. Beatrice will soon be a name of the past, since it is now being torn apart piece by piece, allowing the raiders, who followed the advice of their Wall Street mentors, to walk away with an estimated profit of over $2 billion. Is this what the hotshots at Salomon Brothers and Drexel Burnham learned at Harvard Business School? If so . . . well, reach your own conclusion.

Or what about those corporate chiefs who do not fight back? Many offer to just step out of the way of the asset strippers, provided they are paid off in the form of "golden parachutes," which often amount to $10 million, even $20 million, amounts simply handed out to executives who were in the process of running their corporation into the ground.

Black Monday has brought much of this activity to a halt. But we, all of America, are left with the legacy of the runaway greed of a few. They will just walk away when recession begins next year. But we will now have to live through a recession that will be much more serious and develop much more quickly than would have been the case had it not been for the ill-fated overleveraging of corporate America that Wall Street engineered.

Were our future just to hold this "Seidman cascade of corporate bankruptcies," it would hardly be reason to get overly concerned. We went through similar experiences in the nineteenth century with regularity, and always came out of them within six to nine months. The problem is that there is a much larger complex of financial difficulties out there of an *international* nature that recession in the United States could greatly magnify and bring to the acute stage. I am talking about the Third World debt situation. To put this "international" threat into perspective relative to the "domestic" one: whereas the amount of LBO-related junk bonds currently outstanding comes to less than $150 billion, the amount of highly suspect Third World debt currently exceeds $1 trillion.

Since it is always the debtors who get hit hardest when hard times come, it will be these debtor *nations* that are going to get into trouble immediately following the beginning of recession in the United States. At this stage we could be faced not only with a cascade of domestic corporate bankruptcies, but now also with a process of massive debt default in the Third World. And the reason will be the same: a sudden disappearance of the cash flow necessary to cover massive interest payments arising out of overleveraging. Where Safeway is an example of an overleveraged corporation that could be devastated by recession in 1989, Brazil and Mexico are the world's prime examples of overleveraged nations that could be brought to their financial knees very quickly when the good times end.

How would this come into play? And who would be next on the hit list? Logically, it would be the institutions that have *over*lent to those *over*leveraged corporations and nations, such as the money-center banks in the United States. How would that play out? And where will it all end?

The Convergence Theory

Looking at the economic and political factors that face us in 1988 and early 1989, in particular the overleveraging of corporations and nations, I have arrived at what I call the Convergence Theory. To put it simply, I see six events that will converge, one reinforcing the effect of the other, culminating in a financial crisis of unprecedented proportions in the postwar world.

Event #1

While nonspectacular in itself, the end of the marvelous Reagan recovery will be the first step toward recession. This event will surprise no one, since the leading economic indicators issued by the Commerce Department will have moved down three months in a row in the fall of 1988, warning that recession is imminent. The 1988 Christmas retail sales, when toted up in early January of 1989, will be off appreciably, confirming that consumer spending has finally turned down. The recession of 1989 is about to begin.

Event #2

The second event in this convergence theory is the inauguration of the new President of the United States. Is he a Democrat or a Republican? And will it matter?

Where the onset and initial severity of the '89 recession is concerned, the party affiliation of the next President won't matter a whit. The events that will take place in the first half of 1989 will have been predestined before he took office. In fact, the shape of things to come in 1989 is for the most part already determined today, well before the November 1988 election. For it is the cumulative effect of the first seven and a half years of the Reagan presidency, not the last few months, that will determine our immediate future and those conditions which the next President will inherit when he assumes office on January 20 of next year.

But as I size up the candidates for both political parties, I believe that the public will decide that a change of guard is necessary and elect a Democrat.

Where the party affiliation of our next President *will* make a difference is in regard to the nature of his response to the '89 recession, especially when it starts to get nasty. And his policy response will to a very substantial degree determine our investment response. Rather than remaining completely ambivalent on this very important factor in our financial future, let's assume that the next President of the United States will be a Democrat, one somewhat left of center.

Event #3

A sudden worsening of the nation's economic outlook will start as the cascade of domestic bankruptcies à la Seidman begins. By March it is becoming increasingly obvious that this will not be "recession as usual" but something definitely worse.

The consumer, sensing this, now *really* begins to pull in his horns. A lot of economists had expected him to do so much earlier, i.e., after the Panic of '87 on Wall Street. But he didn't, because for the vast majority of Americans, Black Monday had no *immediacy*. Most of his holdings of stocks were *indirect*, via mutual funds, or even more indirect, via his participation in a company pension fund. Where the latter is concerned, most Americans don't even have a clue about how and where their pension money is invested, and since sixty-five is still a way off for most of them, they don't care that much about what happens on Wall Street on a month-to-month or even year-to-year basis. As long as everything looks as if it is going to turn out all right in the long run, when he will need his pension money, his attitude and buying habits stay more or less the same. Which, contrary to almost all predictions, is exactly what happened on Main Street following the October 19 panic on Wall Street.

The American consumer's attitude might have changed dramatically in 1987 had the stock market crash not been totally contained to the market participants; had it spread through the investment banking community to the commercial banks, affecting his ability to extend credit to him, the story might have been quite different. But it stayed contained, and the consumer remained confident.

In early 1989 it will be different—because now *employment* and *paychecks* throughout America will be on the line. When somebody in San Jose read that a Yuppie lost his job on Wall Street in 1987, that was one thing; when his next-door neighbor gets laid off by Safeway or United Airlines or Macy's in March 1989, that will be another.

The response will come in the form of a sudden acceleration in the contraction of consumer spending as unemployment starts to spread from the weak companies, which got into trouble first because of their overleveraged financial positions, to solid companies such as General Motors and Apple Computer and their suppliers, causing consumer confidence to weaken still further as fear begins to spread throughout the land.

Event #4

As the United States sinks abruptly into recession, within a remarkably short time it starts to pull Europe and Hong Kong and Japan down with it. We saw what happened to the stock markets of the world in the week following Black Monday. New York, which plunged 22.6 percent that day, ended the month of October down only 10.6 percent from its pre-Panic level. Now look what happened around the world:

COUNTRY	% DECLINE OF STOCK MARKET OCTOBER 19–30, 1987
AUSTRALIA	43.0
HONG KONG	41.3

COUNTRY	% DECLINE OF STOCK MARKET OCTOBER 19–30, 1987
SINGAPORE	39.1
MEXICO	34.7
NORWAY	28.8
SPAIN	23.1
BRITAIN	21.0
SWEDEN	19.8
SWITZERLAND	18.6
WEST GERMANY	16.2
CANADA	15.9
ITALY	15.7
JAPAN	12.0

In every single case the declines around the world exceeded those in New York, and often by a whopping margin. Why this "knee-jerk" reaction? As *The Economist* pointed out, "Information now flows almost instantaneously between markets which makes movements more rapid and often more extreme. Global markets mean global euphoria and global panics." Barton Biggs, chairman of Morgan Stanley Asset Management, agreed: "It was global panic. The degree of linkage around the world has been devastating."

Linkage. And because that same linkage extends to almost every facet of global economic activity, what happened globally following the panic of the American stock market will in the highest probability be repeated following the crash of the American economy. The economies of Europe and much of Asia will quickly follow us into recession.

And just as the declines in foreign stock markets precipitated by the Panic of Wall Street were extraproportional to the decline in stock prices in the United States, so also the effects of American recession in 1989 could end up being more devastating abroad than they will be at home. And again it is because of linkage, and the fact that the *strategic link* in the global system of economics and finance is the United States.

During the past four years the United States of America has been the *sole* engine of growth for the entire developed world. In the previous two decades it had been a three-engine world, with Germany through its economic growth pulling all of Europe behind it, and with Japan doing the same for much of Asia. Since 1984, however, over 50 percent of all economic growth has, directly or indirectly, come from the United States: directly in the form of the vast economic expansion under the Reagan administration, which created over 12 million new jobs in this country, while employment in both Europe and Japan was stagnating; indirectly in the form of the economic stimulus that our country provided to the rest of the world as a result of our enormous trade deficit. The $170 billion trade deficit, a product of excess demand in the United States spilling across our borders, meant that this huge amount of American purchasing power was stimulating output in Germany and Japan, instead of in Detroit or Pittsburgh. We have been supporting the whole bloody world!

And we simply can no longer afford to do so. The recession of 1989 is going to signal our forced retreat from being the world's economic benefactor—not a few would say the world's economic patsy. As unemployment rises from 6 to 7 to 8 percent, incomes in the United States recede proportionately, and so also will our imports of Swiss watches and Hong Kong textiles and German machine tools and British scotch. When you lay American recession on top of the massive dollar devaluation that has already occurred, what has already happened to Porsche's exports to the Yuppies will now happen to Mercedes' exports to the American rich and Honda's exports to the American middle class. This, combined with the depressing effect on consumers around the world brought on by the spread of global uncertainty about the economic future, will mean that Europe's economy will turn downward almost immediately, and Japan's slide back to zero growth will follow within a matter of months.

Theoretically, the global spread of the next American recession could have perhaps not been avoided, but it certainly could have been mitigated, had West Germany and Japan responded to repeated pleas by the United States Treasury in 1987 and 1988 to spur growth in their economies through more expansive fiscal and monetary policies, increasing domestic consumption and thus reducing the risk of overreliance on the huge American market for their products. Had they done this, in 1989 their economies would have been on the rise, and the global shock of a sudden American downturn could have been considerably lessened.

But they chose not to go this route. For as Jeffrey Garten, a New York investment banker and former deputy director of the State Department's policy planning staff, pointed out in a post-Panic article in the New York *Times*, "The objectives of the three nations are incompatible. The United States wants growth to offset the crash, and seems willing to accept some inflation in the process as well as a declining dollar. Bonn wants, above all, stable prices and is prepared to sacrifice growth. Tokyo wants low prices, growth and, with an eye on its exports to the United States, a stable dollar-yen relationship. Something has to give."

Well, what will give in 1989 is first the American economy, and then theirs. Net result: global recession throughout the industrial world.

Event #5

Now we phase in the sudden financial collapse of the Third World. And we will focus upon two nations, Brazil and Mexico, not merely because they are the largest debtors, both owing over $100 billion, but also because they represent the two classes of Third World debtor nations: those *without* oil, like Brazil, and those *with* oil, like Mexico.

But before we look at these two key nations in particular, let's go back to the origins of the problem to see how they—and now we—got into this mess in the first place: a mess that we managed to live with for well over a decade but one that has now become acutely threatening in March/April of 1989.

As with so many recent economic woes in the modern world, it started with oil. In 1973, when the price of oil went from $2.00 to $10 a barrel, a lot of poor countries that happened to have oil got rich overnight—like Saudi Arabia and Kuwait and Venezuela—while a lot of other lesser-developed countries (LDCs) like Argentina, or Zaire, or Brazil, those without oil, got poor or at least poorer. The former group was piling up oil income much faster than it could spend it, while the latter countries were suddenly paying energy import bills five times the size they had been used to, draining even further their limited foreign exchange resources.

The obvious solution would have been for the *rich* LDCs with oil to lend some of their surplus dollars to the *poor* LDCs. But that would have been too logical. Plus the fact is that the Arabs are not dumb. Why risk lending money to potential basket cases?

Enter creative financing, masterminded by the hot-shots from Chase Manhattan, Bank of America, Citibank, and Manufacturers Hanover. Lend the money to us, they told the fellows in Riyadh, and *we* will lend to the potential basket cases.

Sovereign loans are what they called them. And their reasoning was this: people go broke; companies go broke; even banks, God help us, sometimes go broke—but countries *never* do. Right? How safe can you get? And who else can borrow billions at one crack and thus save you the enormous amount of paperwork that comes when all you are lending is millions? Only countries, that's who. So let's borrow from the Saudis and lend to the potential basket cases and make a few points in between—make a few millions, or ten millions, in profit—on the transaction.

The immense supply of surplus petrodollars created its own demand in the form of sovereign loans. Oil money poured into the banks from OPEC countries and the men in their pin-striped suits got onto Pan Am and headed for darkest Africa and remotest Latin America, searching for sovereign nations who would take some of those billions off their hands—at a few percentage points over the rate they were paying the Arabs, plus enormous front-end fees. The New York commercial bankers had found a new way to rake in huge profits while expending only a limited amount of time and effort. In the next decade it was the New York *investment* bankers who did exactly the same by charging obscene front-end fees for arranging LBO financing through the issue of junk bonds. What a better world it might have been without so much help from these guys!

In any case, the pinstripes found their customers quick enough. Costa Rica took a billion; then Peru took two; Argentina escalated to ten. Then the bankers figured: Hell, if Argentina was good for $10 billion, Brazil should be able to handle at least $20 billion.

And so it went between 1973 and 1978. By the end of that period, bank loans from the developed world to the LDCs had gone from almost zero to over $250 billion.

Then came the second oil "shock" of 1979. The price of crude, which had seemingly stabilized in the $10 range, suddenly zoomed to $20 a barrel, then $30, then $40. The OPEC surpluses quadrupled. There was not an energy expert on earth, including myself, who was not firmly, indisputably, irrevocably forecasting that $60 and then $80 and then $100 a barrel were inevitable, probably by as early as the mid-1980's. Which meant that there would be money galore gushing out of the Arabian peninsula into the hands of the world's bankers *ad infinitum.* So the bankers scrambled around the world ever faster, lining up takers willing to pledge their countries, maybe now for the tenth time, as collateral for yet another sovereign loan. As a result, during the next two years the banks *doubled* their lendings to the LDCs—bringing the grand total to over half a trillion dollars.

Then came a new wrinkle. Heretofore the oil-producing LDC's had been the *suppliers* of funds to the banks, and the non-oil-producing LDCs had been the *borrowers* of the same funds from the same banks. Beginning in 1979, that changed: Nigeria, Venezuela, and Mexico—oil-rich nations if ever there were such—suddenly decided that if the price of oil was inevitably headed toward $100 a barrel, then they might as well lie back and enjoy it. Emulate the Yankee formula for success: buy now, pay later.

So they embarked upon massive development programs financed fifty-fifty cash/debt—one half still coming from their current oil income, the other half now financed by the external borrowing of dollars from the banks of the developed world. Mexico borrowed $91 billion; Venezuela borrowed $36 billion; Indonesia got $22 billion; Nigeria $10 billion. As a result Mexico became the fastest-growing nation on earth; Venezuela was second.

And as new loans continued to pour into Brazil, heading toward a grand total of $110 billion, that country became number three in the world's growth sweep-stakes as it, too, prospered as never before. The Brazil-ians began building state-of-the-art manufacturing facil-ities, based to a large degree on very expensive imported German technology, and started exporting steel; then shoes; then automobiles; then even aircraft, both civil-ian and military. When you added such exports to Brazil's traditional exports of coffee and sugar and or-anges, there could be no question—none whatsoever—that Brazil was finally on a roll that would allow it to earn more than enough dollars not only to fully service its debt, but to pay it all back on schedule by the year 2000. Ditto for Mexico, on the basis of its oil exports alone.

The New York bankers were jubilant: they had pulled off the financial coup of the century.

And then came the first oil glut at the beginning of the 1980's. The oil price, instead of soaring from $40 a barrel to $60 a barrel, as everybody said it would, went back down to $35, then $32, then $29. The projected oil income of the oil-producing LDCs collapsed along with the price. The resulting problem was compounded by the fact that those countries had borrowed short-term even though the development projects they were financing were, by definition, of a long-term nature. Thus in 1982 alone Mexico was committed to repay the banks of the developed world $29.2 billion. In August of 1982 the Mexicans had to come to New York and tell the bankers who had been assembled there by the Federal Reserve that they could not pay. They were going to have to go into default. Mexico had suddenly run out of money.

As we know, Paul Volcker and the Fed saved the day by reliquifying Mexico, the United States, and the world. But now a new age had dawned: the age of rescheduling. Since there was no way that Mexico could even begin to pay off any of the principal on due dates, the banks simply "rescheduled" them, postponing repayments due in 1982 to 1985, then, when 1985 arrived, postponing them yet again to 1987. When it appeared that Mexico might not even be able to pay the interest on these loans (which would have forced the American banks to write down their value and admit to huge losses), new loans to Mexico were arranged, the new money being used to meet the interest payments on the old loans on time. The last loan of this type was necessary not that many months ago, one of $14.4 billion, provided to Mexico just last fall by a consortium of lenders including the IMF, the World Bank, and all the large commercial banks in the United States.

But that still should have left Brazil in good shape, shouldn't it? After all, that country did not rely to such a degree on a single export, oil, and on one subject to wild price fluctuations. It now had a broadly diversified export base, ranging from basic commodities and food-stuffs to jet aircraft, meaning that as long as the export markets for these products remained prosperous—espe-cially the markets in the United States, which takes over half of Brazil's exports—then at a bare minimum it could at least always pay the interest.

Wrong. Despite the high prosperity reigning not only in the United States, but also in Europe and Japan, i.e., in *all* of Brazil's principal export markets, in February of 1987 Brazil ran out of dollars and was forced to de-clare a moratorium on all interest payments. Only after the American banks granted it a new loan of $4.5 billion in November 1987 was it able to resume interest pay-ments on its $110 billion debt. The first transfer of funds from Brazil to an American bank occurred in the final days of December of last year. The world's bankers had once again dodged the bullet. However, in January of 1988, Brazil declared it would not resume full interest payments until new loans were guaranteed by the banks.

But now, as bailout followed bailout, the question was increasingly asked: if Brazil—and Peru and Argentina and the Philippines—needed such bailouts during *good* times in the United States, what in the world was going to happen when the music stopped and *bad* times set in north of the Rio Grande?

Well, now we are at precisely that point in our scenario. In early 1989 the music *is* stopping. The merry-go-round *is* grinding to a halt. The circular flow of dollars *is* beginning to dry up. As the American consumer pulls back, he consumes less and less Brazilian coffee and sugar and shoes, causing Brazil's dollar earnings to rapidly decline. But Brazil must still continue to buy oil abroad, and to pay for it in dollars. Ditto for machine tools and grain and copper. So it must now begin to deplete its meager dollar reserves in order to keep the domestic economy going. Sensing that a new crisis is brewing (as it has so often in the past), the rich Brazilians once again start to yank their money out of Brazil and put it in a safe-haven bank in Miami or Geneva, depleting Brazil's dollar reserves even further. So now, in April of 1989, just sixteen months after it resumed its interest payments to the American banks, Brazil must again go into default.

Unfortunately, it is at precisely this juncture that Mexico is also going to come back to haunt us, *really* haunt us this time—and Mexico ranks right up there with the Soviet Union and Japan as one of *the* nations that have overriding importance where the future strategic interests of the United States are concerned— since it is once again headed toward international bankruptcy. As in August of 1982, so now also in April of 1989, Mexico had suddenly run out of money, and it has no choice but to follow Brazil into default. And the reason for this new financial crisis in Latin America is again oil. As we have seen, it was the unprecedented rise in the price of oil in 1979 that enticed our banks to lend Mexico so much money in the first place. It was a reversal in that price trend, from $40 a barrel back to $28, that triggered the *first* Mexican debt crisis in August 1982. It will be the collapse of the oil price in 1989 that will precipitate the *second* Mexican debt crisis and, because of the convergence of other events, which we have been tracking one by one, will lead to an unprecedented *global* financial crisis.

Event #6

This involves the price of oil dropping to $10 a barrel in early 1989 *and staying there for at least a year.* How probable is this? I'd say the chances are 3 out of 4. The reasons can be found on both the demand and supply side of the global oil equation.

Energy demand had been more or less flat between 1980 and 1988, because of the energy conservation brought on by the oil shock of 1979. This meant that OPEC could sell into a predictable and reasonably firm market during most of the 1980's. No more. For in 1989, for the first time in the decade, the demand for energy will be seriously sinking as a result of the onset of global recession. There is a direct correlation between overall economic activity and the consumption of energy, especially oil and oil products. When one sinks, so does the other.

But the real "problem" for the oil price has always come from the supply side: overproduction. OPEC was originally set up to take care of that "problem." It is nothing other than a cartel designed to limit the output of oil by its member countries to levels that will allow for high prices. Each OPEC member was given an output quota, and if all the members had stuck to it, the price would probably have remained at around $28 a barrel for many years. The problem is that OPEC includes a couple of somewhat loony, renegade members —such as Libya and Iraq—as well as a few rather impoverished nations, like Nigeria and Indonesia. Driven by greed or need, occasionally these members would begin to pump oil in amounts greatly exceeding their quotas. The nation that always stepped in to correct such situations when they arose was Saudi Arabia. It became what was known as the "swing producer." This meant that when a few OPEC members began overproducing, the Saudis would cut back their output to compensate. Soon the threat of a glut would be overcome, the renegade producers could be talked into cooling it for a while, and the price remained stable.

The Saudis could easily afford to do this, since at peak times they were producing as much as 11 million barrels a day. This meant that Saudi Arabia was taking in enough money to buy the equivalent of all the equities listed on the London exchange *every nine months*, according to a calculation made at the time by *The Economist*.

But as the Saudis cut their production back to 9 million barrels a day, then 7 million, then ultimately to 2 million barrels a day, to maintain market equilibrium, their oil income sank drastically. Yet they had to continue to pay for the huge development projects they had under way, ranging from superhighways to airports to hospitals to petrochemical plants. Soon there was a gap between expenditures and income, and to fill it the Saudis were forced to begin drawing down the enormous cash hoard they had built up in the good years. As a result, at the end of 1985 it was estimated that they were down to their last $75 billion. Life, you see, is not easy *anywhere*.

This convinced Sheik Zaki al-Yamani, then oil minister of Saudi Arabia, that enough was enough. He would now teach the rest of OPEC a lesson. This time *he* would flood the market. He did, and the oil price collapsed back to $9.00 a barrel in early 1986. But this episode was very short-lived. King Fahd fired Yamani and brought in a new man who immediately cut back Saudi production. This country had once again assumed the mantle of swing producer.

The result was that the price moved back up to the $20-to-$22-a-barrel range, and it would probably be there to this day had not a new development occurred, one that will have much more deadly consequences for the future price of oil than Yamani's little fling. I refer here to the sudden heightening of the rivalry between the Saudis and the Iranians, a rivalry involving not just the leadership of OPEC, but that of the politics and religion of the Middle East.

Saudi Arabia and Iran have always been the coleaders of OPEC, owing to the simple fact that they both have the largest potential output capability: Iran can theoretically produce at a rate of 6 million barrels a day; Saudi Arabia, at 12 million, or even much higher. To put this in perspective, all of OPEC today produces 18 million barrels a day. Following the Yamani-created fiasco, both nations agreed that the price should once again be stabilized, under their coleadership, and they did just that.

But then the leaders of Iran, in their madness, sent five hundred of their citizens to Mecca during last year's annual pilgrimage to that holy city of Islam with the mission of starting demonstrations and riots aimed at destabilizing the Saudi regime, opening the way for a spread of their Shi'ite fundamentalist brand of Islam to the Arabian peninsula. Not only did the Saudi leadership gun down the Iranians in front of Mecca's main mosque, but soon their King publicly announced that a permanent wedge had been created between the two nations. Cooperation on price was now obviously impossible.

To be sure, despite the irreparable break between these two nations, neither immediately sought to undermine the quota system of OPEC to "teach a lesson" to the other one, to show who was boss, who had more staying power. The reason Iran continued to go the price rather than the volume route—all through 1987 and well into 1988—was that it had no alternative. Given the tanker war in the Persian Gulf, and the constant Iraqi attacks on Iran's principal export terminal on Khark Island, it was impossible for Iran to increase its exports. Therefore, to ensure the highest possible income, which it desperately needed to finance the war, Iran had to go the price route. But imagine what would —no, *will*—happen when the Iran-Iraq war ends. All such constraints on output will no longer exist, and Iran will begin to pump oil to the absolute limit of its capacity, seeking to replenish its war-devastated national treasury.

But why should that war end? The answer is sheer attrition on the battlefield and pure national exhaustion. The battles along the Shatt-al-Arab waterway have thus far resulted in more than a million casualties. In terms of blood spilt, of men killed, the last time we were forced to witness such carnage was during the trench battles of World War I. The Iranians are down to thirteen- and fourteen-year-old boys, which they send in ahead of their more weathered troops, to blow up the minefields, to draw the enemy's initial fire, to be sacrificed in the name of Allah.

The Iraqis are not a hell of a lot better, that's for sure. When all else fails, they resort to gas warfare. As a result, slowly the entire world, even including the Soviet Union, is saying, "A plague o' both your houses." Weapons procurement is getting increasingly difficult for both warring nations. Conditions for the populations in both Baghdad and Tehran are getting worse and worse. All it needs is one last straw—perhaps the natural death of the Ayatollah Khomeini, or the assassination of Iraq's President Saddam—and that will finally be it. The way will have been opened for both sides to declare victory, and to retreat to their original borders on both sides of the Shatt-al-Arab channel, after which a new contest will begin: to see which nation, Iran or Iraq, can export the most oil soonest.

How much can they export? Iran, 6 million barrels a

day; Iraq, 4 million, maybe 4.5 million. How much do they produce and export today? Jointly, maybe half of that. How much does all of OPEC sell today in the world market? Between 16 and 18 million barrels a day —not even OPEC knows exactly, since its members rarely tell the truth to one another. What will happen to the price of oil when that output surges to 20 million or even 22 million, when Iran and Iraq both go the volume route in spades? It will drop like a stone. Unless . . . unless Saudi Arabia once again reassumes the role of swing producer.

Will it? After what happened in Mecca?

No way.

The result will be $10 oil. One further remark. Some of the best oil experts in the world believe that the price of that commodity will sink to that level in 1989 even *without* a total winding down of the Iran-Iraq war. And their reasoning is this: OPEC has a sustainable output capacity of at least 28 million barrels a day. Today it utilizes 60 percent of that capacity. Should the current OPEC quota system continue to break down even further, which is almost a sure bet given the disarray within OPEC's ranks, and should that utilization level rise to 70 or even 75 percent, $10 a barrel would result even were the Iranians and Iraqis to continue slaughtering each other.

That would mean that the situation of Mexico could get very nasty very quickly. For the oil price collapse will come on top of a situation that is already desperate.

For a while, between 1985 and October of 1987, it had looked as if Mexico was well on the way to an impressive economic turnaround. The resurgence had begun when Mexico's government scrapped its policy of sheltering Mexican industry in a protected domestic market and began a successful push for economic growth by exporting manufactured goods. But this comeback came to a screeching halt on October 19, when the panic on Wall Street triggered fears that if the crash was a precursor of recession in the United States—a market that absorbs two thirds of Mexican exports—it would mean that Mexican industry would be caught in a squeeze between a shrinking export market and a still-depressed domestic market, and the whole country could go into the tank.

These fears hit the Mexican stock market like a bomb: overnight, following October 19, that market went from being the world's fastest-rising to its fastest-falling one. During the first nine months of 1987 the Mexican stock index, their equivalent of our Dow Jones, went up 330 percent. Following Black Monday, it plunged 75 percent.

What ensued next was a massive flight of capital, as Mexico's rich interpreted what was happening on their stock exchange to mean that suddenly their country's economic prospects had once again turned bleak. So they began fleeing from the peso, moving into dollars and Swiss francs, transferring their assets from Mexico City to banks in Texas, New York, and Geneva. The Mexican central bank saw its foreign exchange reserves, which had peaked at $15 billion (owing, one must now admit, chiefly to two one-time-only events: the $14 billion bailout we had just given them, and the temporary revival of the price of oil to $22 a barrel), suddenly begin to melt down. When they had dropped to $11 billion, rather than risk an immediate foreign exchange crisis, Mexico's central bank stopped supporting the value of the peso. The next day it plunged 34 percent, and in the months that followed continued to erode in a seemingly never-ending process. Now inflation set in with a vengeance, with prices rising on most basic goods and services almost immediately by 80 percent. By the end of 1987 the annual rate of inflation was up to

143 percent. Yet the government refused to allow wages to increase at nearly the same rate.

The judgment of Mexican novelist Rafael Ramírez Heredia on the situation that existed at Christmastime: "Mexicans have passed from poverty to misery."

But then, right after Christmas 1987, all of a sudden there was a new ray of hope. It took the form of a deal which the Mexican Government proposed to the Morgan Guaranty Trust Company, and which Morgan passed on to the other American banks that were part of the Morgan-led syndicate which had lent Mexico huge sums of money over the years. The proposal was for a bond issue/debt forgiveness exchange. It was designed to alleviate at least partially the staggering carrying costs Mexico faced arising out of its $101 billion external debt, reducing its annual interest payments by $800 million a year. Perhaps this was a modest start, but, it was suggested, it might be just the beginning of much bigger things to come.

For, on the surface at least, the banks would profit equally. It was a win-win proposition.

The basic elements of the proposal were this: if the American banks were willing to forgive approximately $10 billion of the debt owed them, Mexico was willing to replace a second $10 billion of debt with newly issued Mexican bonds, which would be backed by U.S. Government bonds which Mexico would purchase from the U.S. Treasury and which would be held *outside* of Mexico, stored in the vaults of no less than the Federal Reserve Bank in New York. Furthermore, these new Mexican bonds would carry a very good interest rate, 1.625 percent over Libor, the London interbank lending rate, which would make them highly attractive to outside investors, should the banks ever want to sell them. In other words, the American banks were to get $10 billion of highly liquid AAA bonds in lieu of $20 billion debt that was highly illiquid, uncollectable, and *maybe* salable to another bank, or outside investors, for, at most, 50 cents on the dollar.

But hold on. How could Mexico afford to buy those $10 billion worth of bonds from the U.S. Treasury if it had only a grand total of $11 billion in foreign exchange left in the bank back home after the post–October 19 run on the peso?

Here, then, was the catch. Actually, Mexico was buying *zero-coupon* U.S. Treasury bonds, bonds that would *eventually* be worth $10 billion, but only after *twenty years.* Their present-day value? Just what Mexico was going to pay for them: $2 billion.

Which meant that, in reality, Mexico was

1. getting the United States and its banks to agree to Mexico's forfeiting on $10 billion which it owed them and which the banks will now have to write off entirely, eating into their capital and reserves;
2. getting the American banks to accept, in lieu of another $10 billion debt, $10 billion worth of new Mexican bonds, backed by American bonds with a current market value of $2 billion—yes, $2 billion, not $10 billion.

This was the big breakthrough? The panacea? Are you kidding? The only major paper in the United States that saw through it was *The Wall Street Journal*. The other papers, from the New York *Times* to the Washington *Post*, fell for it like a ton of bricks. "The risk," the *Journal* wrote, "is that Mexico would not be able to meet the semi-annual interest payments on its bonds." According to the fine print, the guarantee of the zero-coupon bond will apply only to principal, not to interest.

As the Mexico analyst at Goldman Sachs pointed out, "It doesn't solve Mexico's cash flow problem."

Exactly.

When you are overleveraged, your entire future depends on cash flow. Mexico's cash flow depends, primarily, on the oil price, and, secondarily, on prosperity in the market that absorbs two thirds of all Mexican exports, the United States.

With oil falling to $10 a barrel as it does in our scenario, Mexico's earnings from petroleum exports will be cut in half. With recession in the United States seriously impairing America's ability to absorb Mexico's non-oil exports, Mexico's cash flow will shrink even further. You need only a cheap calculator to figure out now that Mexico is going to run out of money very quickly in 1989. And the first thing to go will be its interest payments to our banks, and most probably also the interest on their fancy newly issued U.S. zero-coupon Mexican bonds.

The United States will now be faced with a double whammy originating in the Third World: both the leader of the LDCs *without* oil, Brazil, and the leader of the LDCs *with* oil, Mexico, have gone into the financial tank simultaneously. Can Venezuela, Latin America's fourth-largest debtor, in hock to the tune of $34 billion, be far behind? After all, it is much more dependent than even Mexico on oil exports. And what about Argentina?

Just the quickest of looks at that country. Argentina is Latin America's third-largest debtor, owing $52 billion, of which $35 billion is owed chiefly to American commercial banks. *The Wall Street Journal* describes the current situation there with these words: "With inflation running at about 20% a month and few signs that the country is coming to grips with its economic problems, there is an increasing likelihood that creditors will cut off new funding and that the country will be forced into declaring a moratorium on its foreign debts." Because without new loans, when recession hits its chief markets in the United States and then Europe, Argentina will become a financial basket case almost immediately, since its cash cushion is only a fraction of Mexico's or even Brazil's: Argentina is down to its last billion dollars in foreign exchange reserves. On any given day, Gordon Getty or Donald Trump probably has more cash on hand than that.

When all four of Latin America's leading nations go under, the rest of that continent will not be far behind.

In my opinion, the organization of a Latin debtors' cartel would only be a matter of months.

Unless Latin America got an immense new infusion of cash. Not $4.5 billion such as Brazil got just a half year ago, or $14.4 billion such as Mexico got at about the same time. No, this time we are talking *real* money.

But in 1989, with financial conditions at home rapidly worsening, will Uncle Sam be willing and able to ship tens of billions of new dollars south of the border to bail out Mexico and Brazil, Argentina and Venezuela, when the rising number of unemployed in Kansas City and Houston and New Orleans obviously has first call on our government's resources?

Hardly.

The convergence and linkage of these six events represents the cause of the Crash of 1989. Before going on to study the impact of these events, let's summarize this Convergence Theory:

- Retail sales slow, confirming the turn downward in consumer spending,

- as the new President of the United States takes office

- at the onset of recession in the United States in 1989, which leads to a cascade of bankruptcies at home, resulting in a precipitous dive in our overall economic activity,

- which immediately leads to recession in Europe and Japan,

- which results in a sudden reduction of imports from the LDCs,

- which leads to renewed debt default by Brazil (now joined by Argentina, Peru, Ecuador, etc.);

- all this coinciding with an "exogenous" event, the end of the Iran-Iraq war, which results in a sudden new surge in the supply of oil coming down the Persian Gulf, just when global energy demand is falling because of global recession,

- which leads to a collapse in the price of oil to $10 a barrel,

- which forces Mexico to default on its debt (and Venezuela, and Nigeria, and Indonesia, etc.).

Four

The Impact

NOW THINGS START TO GET INTERESTING—
because now, finally, we are about to move from *cause* to
effect: from economic cause to financial effect. I have suggested the events that will converge to give us cause.
Now let's turn to the five significant effects that I fore-
see will be produced.

Effect #1

What will all this do to our banks? Put more crudely:
could the combination of all these events put the Bank
of America out of business?

———

Let's start by calculating the exposure of the twelve largest banks in the United States, the so-called money-center banks, in Latin America, the area of their greatest theoretical vulnerability.

To be fair, we must point out that our banks have not just been sitting there waiting for all this to happen. To be sure, they sat there for a hell of a long time, but last year, led by John Reed, the head of Citibank, the largest bank in the United States, they finally began to set aside major reserves against the possibility of some of their Latin American debts proving to be ultimately uncollectible. Citibank grabbed the headlines last summer by announcing that it was setting aside $3 billion in reserves to cover its potential Latin American problems. Then Chase said it was going to set aside an additional $1.6 billion. Bank of America and Manufacturers Hanover chimed in with a billion. But what they didn't tell you is that this still left them with tens of billions of dollars of seriously impaired Latin loans on their books.

How much is left? How seriously are these remaining loans impaired? And if the rest of the "problem" will have to be dealt with, how much of these banks' equity —that which stands between them and Chapter 11— would survive intact?

These are the questions which the banks' large depositors are going to be asking in the middle of 1989, those depositors which supply most of the money-center banks' money, depositors which, because of the size of their deposits, normally *starting* at $1 million, are not insured by the FDIC, but only by the capital and reserves of the banks themselves.

BANKS	LATIN LOANS (BILLIONS)	LATIN LOAN RESERVES (BILLIONS)	NET OUTSTANDING LATIN DEBT (BILLIONS)
CITICORP	$14.0	$3.432	$10.568
BANK OF AMERICA	10.4	1.767	8.633
CHASE MANHATTAN	8.7	2.000	6.700
MANUFACTURERS HANOVER	8.4	1.830	6.570
CHEMICAL BANK	5.9	1.500	4.400
MORGAN GUARANTY	5.4	1.350	4.050
BANKERS TRUST	4.0	1.000	3.000
FIRST CHICAGO	3.1	0.930	2.170
CONTINENTAL ILLINOIS	2.3	0.660	1.540
SECURITY PACIFIC	2.0	0.700	1.300
IRVING TRUST	1.9	0.470	1.430
WELLS FARGO	1.9	0.760	1.140

Next factor in the market value of the Latin American loans that have been left fully intact and *are being currently carried* at full face value on the books of the banks, defined in the table as "Net Outstanding Latin Debt." What are they *really* worth?

ESTIMATED FOREIGN DEBT PRICES
(VALUES ARE EXPRESSED IN CENTS
PER DOLLAR OF FACE VALUE)

ARGENTINA	$.33–.37
BRAZIL	.37–.41
CHILE	.50–.53
COLOMBIA	.72–.76
EQUADOR	.31–.34
MEXICO	.48–.52
PERU	.02–.07
VENEZUELA	.49–.53
BOLIVIA	.13–.16

These estimates were made at the end of 1987 by Shearson Lehman Brothers, and *Grant's Interest Rate Observer*. The Mexican bond issue/debt forgiveness exchange recognized that using market value is a valid appraisal method where our banks' Latin loans are concerned. In fact, since the United States Treasury was a major participant in that $20 billion Mexican debt deal, this approach to "solving" the LDC debt problem—i.e., encouraging the banks to sell or securitize them for what they can get, and then forgive the rest—now had the official recognition of the United States Government, setting, some bankers felt at the time, a very dangerous precedent. And they were probably right. For when you look at the Big Four—Argentina, Brazil, Mexico, and Venezuela—and average the going market discounts on their loans, you end up with only approximately 44 cents on the dollar.

Let's use that number and see what *further* write-offs would be required should the banks be overtaken by events, by a cascade of defaults resulting in a total suspension of interest payments from Latin America, leaving their auditors no choice but to insist that their Latin loans be written down to market. (See the chart on page 126.) Which leads us to the $64 billion question: is the equity of our top twelve banks large enough to absorb such write-offs?

The answer to our last question is an unequivocable no where two of our top five American banks, with total assets of around $350 billion, are concerned. Bank of America and Manufacturers Hanover flunk the test. Their equity capital would be totally wiped out, and more. Citibank, our nation's largest bank, representing another $100 billion in assets, barely passes.

	GROSS LATIN LOANS	MARKET VALUE (44%)	CURRENT BOOK VALUE	REQUISITE ADDITIONAL WRITE-OFF	ESTIMATED COMMON EQUITY	WRITE-OFF (% OF EQUITY)
CITIBANK	14.000	6.160	10.568	4.408	6.726	66%
BANK OF AMERICA	10.400	4.576	8.633	4.057	2.732	149%
CHASE MANHATTAN	8.700	3.828	6.700	2.872	3.101	93%
MANUFACTURERS HANOVER	8.400	3.696	6.570	2.874	2.079	138%
CHEMICAL BANK	5.900	2.596	4.400	1.804	2.106	86%
MORGAN GUARANTY	5.400	2.376	4.050	1.674	4.629	36%
BANKERS TRUST	4.000	1.760	3.000	1.240	2.585	48%
FIRST CHICAGO	3.100	1.364	2.170	0.806	1.306	62%
CONTINENTAL ILLINOIS	2.300	1.012	1.540	0.528	1.134	47%
SECURITY PACIFIC	2.000	0.880	1.300	0.420	3.165	13%
IRVING TRUST	1.900	0.836	1.430	0.594	0.942	63%
WELLS FARGO	1.900	0.836	1.140	0.304	1.823	17%

Effect #2

Now let's look at a scenario. Assume you are the trea-
surer of a Japanese insurance company, or you are running a commercial bank in Tokyo, and you have $100
million on deposit with Bank of America in San Francisco and $200 million with Manufacturers Hanover in
New York. It is July of 1989 and your chief foreign exchange dealer calls you with the news that Mexico had
just declared default. You immediately ask your assis-
tant to put together some numbers quickly, and she
comes up with the same ones we have, highlighting the
lines showing that if the Mexican loans, and then all the
Latin loans, have to be written down to market, the
write-offs would represent 149 percent of Bank of
America's equity; 138 percent for Manny Hanny.

What would you do next? Take a chance and ride it
out?

Or yank!

For the Japanese this situation in the summer of 1989
is not new. They had faced a similar one at the beginning of the summer of 1984. That time, too, the problem
had started in the oil patch, not Mexico's but

Oklahoma's. The bank involved was Continental Illinois. Earlier that year, word had started to circulate that the bank was in way over its head in marginal oil-related loans in Oklahoma. In early June, with the oil price now falling significantly, it was rumoured that these loans were turning sour, one after the other, and that Continental Illinois was going to face an almost immediate hit, at least one billion dollars, maybe two. That would wipe out the bank's entire capital.

On a Wednesday morning in mid-May 1984 the Japanese decided to yank. Within hours the Chicago bank received a series of telexes from Tokyo notifying it that the Japanese would not be renewing their overnight deposits (money that is *literally* here today and gone tomorrow), which amounted to just over two billion dollars. When word of this got around Western Europe, the Germans, then the Swiss and the British, figuring that things must be even worse than they had suspected if the Japanese, of all people, were panicking like this, also began yanking their deposits. By the end of the week this nation's seventh-largest bank was on the ropes. Only an emergency infusion of $13.4 billion, orchestrated by the FDIC, the Treasury, and the Fed, kept the bank open. In retrospect, it was a very, very close call.

The Continental Illinois example should have warned our other money banks that overreliance on foreign depositors who come in with very large (thus uninsured) and often very short-term deposits can be highly dangerous. None heeded that warning. For today every single one of the twelve money-market banks *gets almost half of its deposits from abroad.* In other words, their deposit base today is *just as unstable* as was Continental Illinois's back in 1984.

This phenomenon is relatively new for our banking system. It used to be that all enjoyed the safety inherent in numbers: they got their money through widespread branches from tens of thousands of workers, farmers, businessmen, all Americans—none, at least in recent times, prone to panic where their bank is concerned. Their behavior had its origins in the Great Depression, when ten thousand banks closed their doors permanently, taking their depositors' money down with them. Out of that calamity rose the Federal Deposit Insurance Corporation, which has insured every small deposit in every American bank ever since, with the limit now up to $100,000.

Starting about twenty years ago, a growing number of big banks found a simpler way of raising money:

rather than getting nickels and dimes from thousands of customers through a retail banking system, they decided to go the wholesale route and get millions, even tens of millions, in the form of single large deposits from a few . . . like our Japanese insurance company and bank. The resulting reliance on huge deposits, collectively representing tens of billions of dollars, which *each* of our money-center banks in essence "buys" in Europe or Asia has meant that our big banks no longer have the protection of safety in numbers, and it has also meant that the foreign depositors who now supply them with nearly half—yes, half—their funding no longer have the protection of the FDIC.

The last point is absolutely key. For the decision facing the Japanese once again, this time in the summer of 1989, whether "to yank or not to yank," relates to the risk that maybe *this* time the U.S. Government will *not* take care of all depositors, big or small, insured or not insured, as they did in 1984. This time, maybe, the U.S. Government might choose to stick to the letter of the law, meaning that every depositor having more than $100,000 on deposit with *any* bank—be it Bank of America or some two-bit bank in Wyoming—will now be left out in the cold. There have been recent examples of the

FDIC doing precisely that. Just one of the increasing number of examples: when a small bank, Centennial Savings, went broke in the community where I live in California last year, over four hundred large depositors lost their money.

Knowing this, what would you do if you had a $1 million CD at one of these banks in a situation like this? I suspect that even some very good patriotic Americans might go to the bank and get their money out . . . and gladly pay that "penalty for early withdrawal."

In my scenario, the Japanese do the same. They yank. And as the sun rises soon thereafter in Western Europe, the telexes start to come into our money-center banks from Germany, from Holland, from Britain: same thing. We are right back where we were in the summer of 1984, but with one major, even fundamental, difference: *then* it was a *single-bank problem*, Continental Illinois. Now it is a *systemic bank crisis.*

Where does the money flee to? Barclays Bank in London, Mitsubishi Bank in Tokyo, Amro Bank in Amsterdam, and an awful lot heads for the ultimate haven during times of financial havoc, Switzerland, to Crédit Suisse in Geneva, to the Union Bank of Switzerland in Zurich, to the Swiss Bank Corporation in Basel.

Effect #3

And at the same time as foreign money is fleeing the banks, it begins to flee the U.S. bond market. As U.S. Government bonds are dumped, causing interest rates in New York to rise—no, to *spike*—the stock market gets hit by a massive wave of selling reminiscent of October 19, 1987. And although the action starts in New York, it is soon picked up in Chicago, on the futures market, and before the day is over, it is again the big institutions— fewer than ten of which dominate futures trading in stock indexes in Chicago—that cause a total market collapse. For as they sell the indexes ahead of the drop in the real stocks that are components of these indexes, trying to protect their huge portfolios amounting often to billions of dollars, the psychological situation worsens. This leads to an accelerated selling of stocks in New York and a further acceleration in the selling of the index futures in Chicago, as the institutions continue to try to "stay ahead" of the worst. It was this sort of thing that caused at least the last 200 points of the 500-point drop on October 19, 1987. This phenomenon resurfaced on January 8, 1988, when the market fell by

140 points in one session. Again, the last 70 points of that drop could be directly attributed to institution-led futures trading in Chicago. In the Crash of '89, the Dow drops 320 points, which, in percentage terms, just about equals the world's record set not even two years earlier.

A footnote. In the White House study of the October 19 panic, the so-called Brady report, one of the recommendations aimed at preventing future panics in the stock market involved making trading on stock index futures much more difficult, or at least prohibitively expensive, by stipulating high margin requirements in Chicago. The flaw in this is that, as we have already seen, securities markets are now global, not national. National restrictions on futures trading would merely drive it abroad, to London and Tokyo, just as national restrictions led to the creation and eventual evolution of the Eurodollar market, now a $2 trillion business that is done chiefly out of London, rather than in New York, where it logically belongs.

Effect #4

Back to the Crash of '89 and, this time, the dollar. It is now in free fall, as foreign investors are all trying to get out of it at the same time—those that are fleeing the money-center banks plus those that are fleeing both the bond and the stock markets in New York. The Fed, and the other major central banks around the world, intervene initially, trying to prop it up, but with their billions on the buy side trying to act as a counterforce to tens of billions on the sell side, they soon recognize the futility of such efforts, and give up. The dollar falls to 100 yen, 120 Swiss francs, 140 DM. The British pound Sterling is up to 2.20.

Effect #5

Before the next few days are over, the Dow Jones is down to 1,095, the dollar is worth 95 yen, and interest rates have gone absolutely bonkers in New York: the long bond yield is up to 15 percent, the prime, 18 percent. To be sure: *not a single money-center bank has been allowed to fail*—but only because the Fed has reliquified them on a scale never before seen. It took $13.4 billion to rescue one bank, Continental Illinois, back in 1984. In 1989, in order to rescue the system, or at least the money-center banks at the core of that system, the Fed will have to pour in over $40 billion. This involves an unprecedented jump in money supply, which also leads to an unprecedented jump in inflationary expectations, and still more dumping of bonds, pushing dollar interest rates still higher.

The Crash of '89 has now reached its nadir, and in the days that follow, it leaves the United States exhausted and more fearful of the future than at any time since the 1930's.

Is it now going to be followed by "the Great Depression of the 1990's," as was suggested by a recent bestseller? Or will the Crash of '89 have a different ending? Before examining those issues, let's discuss what you should be doing with your money:

1. before the Crash of '89, and
2. immediately following it.

Crash and Recovery Strategies

Regarding our pre-Crash strategy, you should recall that the Mexican default, the subsequent run on our banks by foreign depositors, and the ensuing collapse of our securities markets across the board had their origins, at least partially, in the recession that will begin at the beginning of 1989. Unemployment, which will start at just above 6 percent—one of the most admirable legacies of the Reagan administration—begins to rise in February, and by June is already up to 7.5 percent, according to my scenario. Construction is at the lowest level in eight years by the beginning of the summer of 1989; ditto for automobile sales. Capital spending on new plant and equipment will have fallen out of sight. The collapse in the price of oil, that other major factor leading to the Mexican default and its aftermath, has also hit *our* oil patch. Its effect, coming on top of the general national economic malaise, means that Texas, Louisiana, Oklahoma, and Colorado are being hit especially hard. The combined effect of all this will cause continual erosion in the stock market in 1989 even prior to the midsummer crash, as the Dow slips first 100, then 200, then 250 points. But since the demand for credit is now diminishing in this recessionary atmosphere, interest rates have also been coming down. To be sure, by only by a little over 1¹/₂ percent, since it will still be necessary to keep dollar interest rates high enough by international standards to ensure that foreign money keeps coming into our government bond market. Nevertheless, down they will come from their mid-1988 highs near 10 percent to a recession-induced range of 8¹/₂ percent, meaning that at least *one* financial market will remain firm during the first half of 1989, the *bond* market.

Bonds

Now to the pre-Crash 1989 investment strategy. If you recall, I suggested that in the middle of 1988, before all this started to happen, you put half of your investable funds in U.S. Treasury long bonds (locking in, let us hope, a yield near 10 percent) and keep the other half liquid, in bank CDs (under $100,000 per bank), or in money market accounts at banks.

The late spring of 1989 is the time to change tactics. It is the time to sell those bonds. You should be selling into a strong market, and could expect to make, interest and capital gain included, 20 percent on your bond investment. I would suggest that you put the proceeds into a money market account, and, for the moment, I would then sit tight in essentially a 100 percent near-cash position.

There are only two exceptions to this: one would be

some options on index futures in Chicago, and the other would be gold.

Options

The options/futures play would be high-risk, only for people with some money they can afford to gamble away. I am suggesting that you buy a few *put* options on future contracts of one of the stock indices. I stress, *options* on futures, *not* the futures themselves. Because with options you can lose only what you put up in the form of the option premium. With futures you can lose everything, including your shirt and, as some found out on October 19, 1987, a whole lot more. In fact, as a private investor I would never ever fool around with any index or commodity futures. The record clearly shows that 85 percent of all speculators who do so eventually get wiped out by margin calls.

Back to the somewhat "safer" speculation—using options on those futures. The futures contract I prefer, because it is most widely traded by the big institutions and thus most liquid, is that on the S&P 500. Each contract represents a basket of 500 stocks worth approximately $120,000. The option approach works like this:

you buy a "put" option on a futures contract that gives you the right to sell that contract at a predetermined price at a future date, say six months in the future—i.e., in our example, December 1989—at, say, 225 versus a current price of 255. You put up $3,000 per contract. You are betting that the stock market as a whole is going to go down by at least 10 percent at some time during those six months, pulling your basket of shares down with it, allowing you to sell your option at a profit. If, before the option period ends, the market collapses again, you will make approximately $500 for each point of decline in the S&P 500 below 225. If you are a dreamer, you will look up what happened following October 19, 1989. That index dropped from 335 to 181, meaning that on your lousy $3,000 investment you would have gotten back $75,000. Then again, if the Dow had gone to 3,000, instead of dropping to almost 1,700, you would have lost your $3,000 *but no more.* From the point of view of the risk/reward ratio, let's put it this way: it's a lot better than anything Las Vegas has to offer.

Gold

God knows I'm not a gold bug, but buying some gold in the spring of 1989, or even earlier, will be hard to resist. A crash of the proportions I have described in 1989 would create *global* fears that would dwarf those created by that panic in 1987. There would be a mass mistrust of *all* banks, *all* currencies, logical or not. Under such circumstances people, through the ages, have turned to the money substitute gold, in the belief that it is the ultimate store of value. I think that is precisely what will happen again, pushing the gold price above $600 an ounce. I would therefore buy it in early 1989, *and plan to sell it almost immediately following any financial panic.* For after that the fundamentals will again take over. And they suggest that higher gold prices will evoke a tremendous surge of new gold supplies, not just in South Africa, but especially in the United States, Canada, and Australia. So the gold play would involve a quick, *speculative* in and out.

Stocks

Now from gambling back to investments. If, as I hypothesize, recession and financial crisis are going to drag the Dow back to below 1,200 in 1989, this could represent the best stock-buying opportunity left in this century. This level of the market would mean that from the point of view of price-earnings ratios, yields, and market versus book value—already discussed in this book—you would be very definitely in buy territory, just as the market was so obviously in sell territory in August/September/October of 1987, when it was flirting with 2,700. Echoing my previous analysis of these fundamental ratios, "buy territory" in the market was recently defined in a study by Leon Cooperman, a partner in charge of investment research at Goldman, Sachs & Co. His study of ten market bottoms since June 1949 showed that, on average, the market bottomed out when stocks were selling about 11 times projected earnings, when dividends were yielding 5 percent of the stock price, and when stocks were selling at approximately 1.3 times book. In mid-1989, after the second panic in two years, if my projection of a Dow in the 1,100-to-

1,200 range is correct, you will beat these "buy" points in every instance.

What to buy?

I believe the best investment is in Basic America; the companies which, taken together, represent the industrial foundation of this nation. Because shortly after the Crash of '89, when we will reach the low point of the recession of '89, what will lie ahead is the rebuilding of this nation's economy. And that will involve—will *have* to involve—less consumption and more production. That means a sudden surge of demand for capital goods, demand which will begin at the nadir of the '89 recession, and carry through well, well into the last decade of this century.

In searching for the best of the best of such companies, a further criterion must be added. Not only should they be in the top rank of capital producers in the United States, but they should also be well positioned in foreign markets, poised to take full advantage of the final massive devaluation of the dollar that will be part and parcel of the Crash of '89.

A portfolio of such stocks, by industry, should include:

INDUSTRIAL ELECTRONICS	Data General Corp. Hewlett-Packard Co.
CHEMICALS	Dow Chemical Co. Union Carbide Corp.
PACKAGING	Stone Container Corp. Union Camp Corp.
ALUMINUM	Aluminum Co. of America (Alcoa) Reynolds Metals Co.
HEAVY EQUIPMENT	Caterpillar Tractor Co.
RAILROAD CARS	Trinity Industries
HYDRAULICS	Trinova Corp.
AND JUST ON PRINCIPLE	IBM Corp.

How much should you put into stocks? At least half of your investable funds, and you will have a lot to invest, since you came through the crash almost 100 percent liquid (with the exception of some gold and that very profitable little play in the options market in Chicago, which you, I hope, liquidated immediately following the Panic). I would suggest that you then take another one quarter of your funds and *re*invest in bonds, trying to catch the bond market at the nadir of the across-the-board crash in the securities markets, the one that had caused the spike of all spikes in interest rates. As panic ends, and recession begins to recede, so will all interest rates. Theoretically, you would now begin one of the great joyrides of all times in the bond market, closely resembling that which occurred between the summer of 1982 and the beginning of 1986, as long-term interest rates fall from 15 percent plus immediately following our '89 panic, to 7 percent two years later, to maybe 5 percent two years after that.

Real Estate

The final investment to be undertaken at this time, if you've got any money left over, or in lieu of stocks and bonds if you are young, is real estate, especially residential real estate: houses, condos, apartment buildings. A panic of the proportions I have described, coming in the middle of a recession, will mean that such properties will be marked down 20 to 25 percent. People caught in the downward vortex of the securities markets will have to sell: savings & loans will be forced to foreclose as never before in recent times as unemployment surges. Cash will be king in real estate.

Real estate's future value will, however, depend upon

how quickly we come out of the depressed economic conditions of 1989, and how far into the future the subsequent recovery extends.

That brings us back to the outlook for the 1990's. Are we on the brink of a decade of depression or at the beginning of a new period of prosperity?

1990 and Beyond

The Road to Recovery

Five

Out of Recession

THERE IS NO GREAT DEPRESSION OF 1990 IN our future. The recession of 1989 is going to be precisely that—*re*cession, not *de*pression. It will begin in February/March of 1989; economic activity in the United States will plunge to a trough immediately following the financial panic in July, reaching bottom in August/September, and then will begin to turn up in the final months of that year.

That would mean a ten-month recession, just about average in length by postwar standards as the following table shows:

THE NINE POSTWAR BUSINESS SLUMPS

PERIOD OF BUSINESS SLUMP	LENGTH IN MONTHS	% DROP IN INDUSTRIAL OUTPUT	PEAK JOBLESS RATE
February 1945– October 1945	8	38.3	4.3
November 1948– October 1949	11	9.9	7.9
July 1953– May 1954	10	10.0	6.1
August 1957– April 1958	8	14.3	7.5
April 1960– February 1961	10	7.2	7.1
December 1969– November 1970	11	8.1	6.1
November 1973– March 1975	16	14.7	9.0
January 1980– July 1980	6	8.7	7.8
July 1981– November 1982	16	12.3	10.7

AND FOR THE RECESSION IN 1989

February 1989– December 1989	10	14.0	9.0

In terms of the plunge in industrial output and the rise to peak unemployment, it will probably most closely resemble the recession that began in late 1973 and our last recession, which began in July 1981. The difference will be that both of those recessions were "U"-shaped—dragging on for sixteen months. The 1989 recession is going to be "V"-shaped, involving a quick violent step down into the trough, and then a rapid recovery from the worst.

We have examined in detail the reasons for the precipitous drop into this recession. Why will we pull out of it rapidly?

The Trade Deficit

The first cause of the rebound will relate to a sudden and massive improvement in our foreign trade deficit. The 20 percent devaluation of the dollar, which will be an integral part of the midsummer Crash of '89, is the final step in an unprecedented devaluation process dating back to September 1985, reducing the dollar's value by 70 percent against those other two key international currencies, the Japanese yen and the German mark.

The final plunge in the dollar in the summer of '89 will represent *the* turning point for the economic fortunes of our nation.

In the years preceding this, the positive effects of devaluation had been masked, camouflaged if you will, by a series of overlapping "J" curves. As you will recall, the "J" curve represents a shorthand way of saying that after a currency devaluation the foreign trade situation always gets worse before it gets better. If that 70 percent devaluation in the dollar had been a one-shot affair, we as a nation would have moved along that "J" curve into positive territory well before 1989. The problem that faces us is that the dollar devaluation process already has and will, I believe, continue little by little, with the result that between 1985 and 1989 the United States will have experienced the effects of a backlog of "J" curves, as each fresh fall in the dollar camouflages the beneficial effects of the previous one. That process will come to an end in the second half of 1989, as the devaluation process also ends. That will mean that the huge backlog of benefits will surface in a massive fashion, meaning that our monthly trade deficit, which probably reached its peak at $17.6 billion a month in late 1987, will be moving quickly toward zero . . .

reaching that target probably late in 1990 or the first part of 1991.

This dramatic turnaround in our foreign trade situation will be enormously helped by the recession itself. For as our incomes and output plummet in 1989, so will our demand for imports. (Remember Porsche.) It will represent an almost classic case of devaluation + recession = a return to balanced foreign trade.

What this will do is pull the rug out from under the protectionists, especially those in the Democratic Party. There are those who believe that such a massive dollar devaluation is so protectionist, in and of itself, that, as Alfred Malabre points out in a widely noted editorial in *The Wall Street Journal*, "it may be the Smoot Hawley" of the 1980's. Where Malabre's thesis goes astray is that the dollar devaluation was done in cooperation with our trading competitors in Europe and Asia. Smoot Hawley, by contrast, triggered a whole series of retaliations of the beggar-my-neighbor policies of the 1930's. This dollar devaluation will definitely not evoke such a retaliatory response.

What this means is that the $170 billion annual leakage in purchasing power will quickly dry up. *Domestic* products will once again be bought in the United States instead of their foreign counterparts in a process called import substitution. Caterpillar tractors, not Kubota's, will once again be bought in Iowa. Furthermore, this final plunge in the international value of the dollar will mean that Caterpillar tractors will once again be competitive in Spain and Morocco and Indonesia, just as they had been in the 1950's and 1960's. As Caterpillar begins to flourish, so will its suppliers, those that provide the company with hydraulics, such as Trinova. Now you see why these companies were included on our post-Panic buy list?

Our international competitive posture is going to be further aided by the fact that, as a result of devaluation, our wages are now far *below* those of many of our competitors. The change within just four years is nothing short of amazing. In predevaluation 1985, American labor costs were 63 percent higher than Japan's and 39 percent above West Germany's. By 1987 statistics compiled by Germany's Dresdner Bank showed that as a result of devaluation American workers had *already then* cost 20 percent less than those in Germany (and Switzerland); 10 percent less than those in Sweden, Holland, and Belgium, and roughly the same as in Japan. When you factor in an additional 20 percent devaluation in

1989, our labor costs will end up 40 percent below those of Germany, 20 percent below those of Japan, and will now, in addition to the countries already cited, also be substantially below wage costs prevailing in Austria, Italy, and France.

Do you see why I'm so optimistic?

If we now add to this a new spirit of hard work rising out of the shock dealt all of us as a result of the 1989 economic and financial crisis, one can anticipate a surge in productivity in the United States that will make the future look even brighter.

A Stumbling Block?

But hold on, you might now interject. What about inflation? Could not a sudden return of double-digit inflation in the United States wipe out all of the gains we derive from dollar devaluation? And is this not likely? After all, if I am right the Fed will have had to put over $40 billion into the banking system to save it from an even greater calamity. Were we not taught by Milton Friedman that six months after such a surge in money supply, inflation *must* increase dramatically.

The answer to all of the above questions is "yes" . . . were the scenario regarding capital flight and looming bank failures to stop where we left off. But it won't. And I'll now explain why.

The massive capital flight from the United States at the height of the '89 Crash will inevitably lead to the following situation: interest rates in New York will spike to levels seldom seen before, except during the Civil War, and again in 1981 when the prime rate rose to 20.5 percent. Due to the liquidity crisis to end all liquidity crises, which will be brought on in the summer of '89 by the unprecedented withdrawal of tens of billions of dollars from the New York money and capital markets by foreigners, a 25 percent prime would not be unlikely, nor a 15 percent yield on long-term U.S. government bonds. (As I already pointed out, this will be the point at which you should re-enter the bond market.) However, one must now also factor in what will be happening *outside* the United States, for instance in Switzerland. Interest rates are *always* low in Switzerland because that country's banks are almost always flush with money. Not only are the Swiss world-class savers, ranking only behind Japan in that respect, but Switzerland has always attracted huge amounts of foreign money, since it has always been regarded as the safest of safe havens: your money is safe from the threat of war, due to Switzerland's neutrality: it is also safe from a potentially even more dangerous threat to your financial future if you've been playing games—namely the IRS, or its counterparts in France, Italy, and everywhere else, due to Switzerland's bank secrecy laws and the fact that its government does not regard dodging taxes as a crime. As a result, Switzerland is sometimes so *overwhelmed* with money that it takes measures to ward off still further inflows from abroad. The reason: more money in circulation could potentially ignite inflation within Switzerland and the Swiss hate inflation. The method used to ward off further inflows (used initially at the time of the traumatic pound sterling devaluation in October 1967): the government requires the banks to *charge* interest on new deposits, instead of *paying* interest as every other bank on earth does.

This will result in short-term interest rates up to 25 percent in New York, and with the banks in Zurich *charging* 2 percent on new deposits, *you end up with an interest-rate differential of 27 percent in favor of New York.*

That differential would suck money off of Mars!

The Return of Foreign Capital

So what would happen next? Slowly, and at first very sheepishly, those tens of billions of dollars, which had fled the United States at the height of the Crash of '89 would start to come back. And yet more would return as the realization sinks in that *only* the money and capital markets of the United States are sufficiently large, sufficiently dynamic, and in the end sufficiently liquid, to absorb those many, many billions that are now floating around the world—money that has been looking, in vain, for a substitute home.

As these funds return, it will be possible for the Fed to gradually withdraw the $40 billion in emergency liquidity that it had injected into the American banking system to preclude the collapse of some of its money center banks. Within a remarkably short time, as was true in 1984 following the near collapse of Continental Illinois, money supply conditions will return to precrisis normalcy. The threat of instant inflation, arising from too much M-1 in circulation, will have disappeared.

A Strong Word of Warning

There is a line of reasoning, one shared by quite a few of our nation's top financial people, that does not so much fear the enemy without—the foreign investors—as much as the enemy within, namely the next President of the United States. What is feared is that if there is a Democrat in the White House in 1989, the odds are unfortunately high that he or she would *overreact* to a sudden precipitous fall in our nation's output of 14 percent, and especially to a sudden, dramatic rise in our unemployment rate to 9 percent. That overreaction would come in the form of massive *reflation* and would involve pumping money and buying power into the system helter-skelter in a headlong effort aimed at preventing the recession of '89 turning into the Depression of 1990. Net result: runaway budgetary deficits that would bring us back to double-digit inflation within a year.

I don't buy this theory, but such a move, while providing some temporary relief, would not solve our lingering economic problems. In fact, if we go back to our table of postwar business slumps at the beginning of

Chapter 5, we find that in most cases there is a coupling of slump periods. Within each coupling there is a one- to three-year lag between recessionary periods. What I am suggesting here is that overreaction on the part of Washington might well put us into a similar situation where we would find ourselves facing another recessionary period—or worse—as early as 1991 or 1992.

As an investor it is imperative that you watch the news carefully during this period. You must be prepared to change strategies and shift your investments quickly if Washington should reflate and we find ourselves in a period of double-digit inflation.

However, I believe that what will actually happen is that due to the "V" shape of the '89 recession, we will already begin to pull out of it *before* the crisis has had time to evoke such a panic response from the White House. And, also due to the "V" shape of the recession, the slump-induced spike in our budgetary deficit will likewise be very short-lived. By the fall of 1989 and into 1990, as economic activity recovers, tax receipts will do the same. And as the number of unemployed starts to recede, so will the extraordinary costs of taking care of them.

In fact, I think that the response evoked by the Crash

of '89 will be *just the opposite of massive reflation*. I think that in public life, as in private, it sometimes takes a huge shock to bring us to our senses. I think that both the White House and Congress will finally be brought to the realization that it is the huge budgetary deficits this nation has been running that will be *the ultimate root cause* of the near financial and economic disaster in 1989. Further, as a result of this shock-induced realization, when recovery gets under way they will finally *seriously* work together to balance the budget in short order. If Democrats control both the White House and the Congress, the job will obviously be easier.

Balancing the Budget

What will it involve? It will *have* to involve higher taxes. One must hope that the emphasis will be on indirect taxes, essentially taxes on consumption. An example of what could be done quickly and without any serious injury to the economy is a tax on gasoline. Every penny tax on gas raises $1 billion in revenue. Keep in mind that currently the federal tax on gas is only $0.09 a gallon, thanks in large part to the power of the oil lobby.

With the oil price down to $12 a barrel, half of what most experts expect it will be in 1989, and with gasoline prices down proportionally, why not slap on a $0.30, then $0.40, then $0.50 tax. That would cover almost one third of the deficit right there. At the same time the price of gas would be only marginally higher—still below the levels of just a few years ago and far below the prices charged in European countries.

And as Peter Peterson, an ex-investment banker and former Secretary of Commerce, has pointed out countless numbers of times, most recently in an article in *The Atlantic Monthly*, entitlements can no longer remain sacrosanct. Automatic increases in social security benefits and government pension benefits, especially where no means test is involved, will simply have to be cut or even temporarily suspended, because of a greater temporary national need: that to bring our nation's finances into equilibrium lest the close call of 1989 be repeated, with the result that *next* time it might lead us into a Depression.

I think that a rise in personal income tax rates will also be necessary. I'm one of the last guys who should be coming out in favor of higher tax rates. But I believe it must be done, and done immediately. It is not necessary to return to pre-Reagan rates, but I do believe that the maximum 28 percent, where we ended up in 1988, will need to be brought back to 35 percent.

This would still leave us as a nation with one of *the* lowest rates in the world as far as personal income tax is concerned. Will such an increase be counterproductive where personal incentives are concerned? Yes, but only marginally, and again it will be a price we will have to pay to achieve a greater national good: financial equilibrium in the 1990's. If a 35 percent rate bothers you, just consider Sweden. It is one of the most prosperous nations on earth, and it has managed to achieve and maintain that status in spite of a marginal tax rate of 75 percent for incomes above 200,000 Skr (Swedish kroner), the equivalent of about $31,000. Norway's taxes are even harsher. In Japan, Britain and Germany they are almost as bad.

Help from an Unlikely Source

And now let me come to a perhaps absurd theory, namely that the man who will ultimately solve our budgetary crisis in the early 1990's will not be the new

President who will be sitting in the White House but a man who already sits in the Kremlin. His name is Gorbachev. If he is to restore the Soviet Union's brand of socialism as a model for anybody else on earth, he must put that nation's economy back into gear. And the only way he can do that is by engineering a massive shift of Soviet resources from guns to butter. That is why he came to Washington on December 7 of last year. That is why he signed the agreement eliminating all medium-range missiles from Central Europe. That is why he invited President Reagan to come to Moscow later this year to sign a follow-up treaty, cutting in half the number of strategic missiles that both nations have deployed. That is why he is willing to discuss asymetrical reductions in conventional forces in Europe, "asymetrical" meaning that he is willing to buy a deal which will require that the Soviets agree to an extraproportional withdrawal of tanks and manpower from Eastern Europe relative to that required of NATO.

Again let me stress, he is not doing this because he wants to help out. He is doing it out of pressing national self-interest.

The ultimate objective is to reduce the percentage of the GNP that the Soviet Union devotes to the defense establishment from the current level of 16 percent to 14 percent, then 12 percent, then 10 percent. My absurd theory is that if this materializes in the early 1990's, and materializes in a verifiable way, then we can begin to cut back our defense budget (of close to $330 billion!) proportionally.

And, *voilà*, a balanced budget not for just a year, but balanced budgets, plural, extending way into the 1990's.

Six

And Beyond Into the 1990's

SHOULD ALL THIS COME TO PASS, AS BOTH
the budgetary and trade deficits come under control,
our need to import savings would disappear, our need
to keep high-dollar interest rates to attract such savings
would likewise disappear, and we would gradually return to something resembling the Eisenhower years: 3
percent growth, 2 percent inflation; 4 percent to 5 percent long-term interest rates. The stage will be set for
the Dow to begin to start moving back to 2,700 and
beyond, levels which *this* time will be fully justified by
the new fundamentals.

In such an atmosphere, there is no doubt that we
could then begin to resolve the Third World debt prob-

lem. This must be addressed now or we risk setting in motion a series of economic circumstance that could lead us once again into a period of recession, perhaps as early as 1992. Lower dollar interest rates will greatly alleviate the situation. But the "solution" will have to come in the form of our banks writing off half of these loans, and our government assuming responsibility for the other half.

Felix Rohatyn, the man who put New York back together again financially by organizing the Municipal Assistance Corporation, has suggested a blueprint for that. It will require that some institution, either an IMF/World Bank subsidiary, or a new one, buy up the remaining commercial banks' debt, remaining after they take the maximum write-offs they can afford, in exchange for long-term low-interest bonds which this institution would issue itself. It would essentially involve taking the Mexican bonds-for-debt swap to its ultimate conclusion. It would take the banks off the hook once and for all, and allow them time to rebuild their capital base, the better to serve the needs of the clients they should have been paying most attention to in the first place, corporate America. As for the debtor nations, they would still have to service the debt that remains, but at much lower interest rates and over much longer periods of time, conditions that only a government-backed entity could grant.

Would this amount to a bailout? Sure it would. But so what. Rather a bailout—where we get the Japanese and European taxpayers to co-share the cost—than a rerun of '89 in '92. How do we get the entire industrialized world to split the cost via the IMF and World Bank? Do you think this is unlikely? Well, remember IMF chairman Jacques de Larosière's intervention at the time of the Mexican debt crisis in 1982, which I described earlier.

Furthermore, pure compassion dictates that we help the people of Mexico and Brazil, of all of Latin America, emerge from the desperate conditions they now face by at least removing from their backs a foreign debt that was for the most part entered into by a greedy and corrupt elite, with much of the money involved ending up in their pockets instead of being used to lift the masses from poverty.

As to the money center banks themselves, there is no doubt in my mind that there will have to be mergers. Irving Trust, First Chicago, Continental, and Manufacturers Hanover will probably not survive such a process. Even though as a Californian it breaks my heart to say so, it would even make sense for Citibank to absorb Bank of America. As *The Wall Street Journal* pointed out in January of this year "like manufacturers over the past decade, banks now face the threat of hostile takeover. Regulators in an era of deregulation look more favorably on bank mergers, and more states are removing their barriers to interstate acquisition. Consolidation in the industry, only just begun, is expected to accelerate." For if America is going to reassume its financial leadership of the world in the 1990's, it will need to have superbanks of its own: banks which can branch on both coasts; banks which will be sufficiently large to compete on an even footing with the giants which have recently emerged, such as Fuji and Mitsubishi in Japan, Deutsche Bank and Dresdner in Germany, Barclays in Britain, and Union Bank in Switzerland.

And what about corporate America? As I have already suggested, I firmly believe that Basic America, the traditional industries upon which our nation was built, will have been given a totally new breath of life by the events preceding and accompanying the Crash of '89, especially the dollar devaluation which will open the way for them, through import substitution, to win back the huge American market which they had almost lost to foreign competition. Furthermore, in the process of catharsis which came in the form of recession in '89, a lot of marginal corporations—yesterday's LBOs will have gone under or been merged into stronger corporations resulting in a leaner and meaner corporate America.

But beyond that, I feel that in the new atmosphere of the 1990's, with both of our deficits finally under control, with interest rates down, with inflation low, in other words with the public sector parameters now benign right across the board, the innovative powers of the United States will come to the fore as perhaps never before. We still have going for us that unique combination of high technology, venture capital, and entrepreneurship that produces wealth out of thin air, a peculiar brand of American magic. The next waves of wealth creation, ones that will resemble that caused by the invention of the transistor forty-one years ago, will come from the economic and financial impulses growing out of the industrial and consumer applications of superconductivity and biotechnology. (You should watch the development in these fields carefully for potential investments.) Risk capital, willing to take a chance on such new industries, will always be abundant in this country. Americans like to shoot for the moon with their money. And there will always be an ample supply of American entrepreneurs willing to bet their professional lives on new ventures in as yet untried fields. For they know that if they succeed, our society will reward them on a scale that would be unimaginable anywhere else.

Which brings me to a final thought. Though many of us may have doubts at times about our economic system, when you travel around the world and then come back home and compare what we've got here to what you've seen out there, how can any of us help but conclude that our capitalistic, free enterprise, democratic system—despite the fact that panics, crashes, and recessions are inherent to it—still represents the best hope for the future of the world—and I mean the *entire* world. So you might make some money in the short run going short in the markets, but you will never make money in the long run by selling America short.

ABOUT THE AUTHOR

Paul Erdman is one of the most sought-after economists in America. He received his Ph.D. summa cum laude from the University of Basel and lectures widely around the country. He writes regular columns for *Manhattan,inc.* magazine and Japan's *Nikkei* magazine. He's the author of *Paul Erdman's Money Book* and six bestselling novels: *The Billion Dollar Sure Thing, The Silver Bears, The Crash of '79, The Last Days of America, The Panic of '89,* and *The Palace.* When not lecturing, trading, or traveling, Paul Erdman lives on a ranch in northern California with his wife, Helly.

THE IACOCCA MANAGEMENT TECHNIQUE
by Maynard M. Gordon

In this age of managers, the undisputed supermanager is Lee Iacocca, America's most famous and popular businessman. Could any other corporate executive have duplicated Iacocca's comet-like rise to stardom and chief spokesman for a moribund car manufacturer? What management techniques enabled him to overcome the many obstacles in his path? How did a businessman become a folk hero?

THE IACOCCA MANAGEMENT TECHNIQUE traces the path of Iacocca's successful approach to corporate executive leadership from his career rise at Ford to his performance of 'mission impossible' at Chrysler. It objectively pinpoints both his achievements and short-comings, from his managerial methods of hiring and firing, to his marketing schemes and dealer relations. It contrasts his style with that of his competitors and finally poses the question: What has he done to insure that the Chrysler he revived will survive after he as gone?

0 553 17281 6

A SELECTED LIST OF NON-FICTION TITLES AVAILABLE
FROM BANTAM BOOKS

While every effort is made to keep prices low, it is sometimes necessary to increase prices at short notice. Corgi Books reserve the right to show new retail prices on covers which may differ from those previously advertised in the text or elsewhere.

The prices shown below were correct at the time of going to press.

ORDER FORM

All Corgi/Bantam Books are available at your bookshop or newsagent, or can be ordered direct from the following address:

Corgi/Bantam Books,
Cash Sales Department,
P.O. Box 11, Falmouth, Cornwall TR10 9EN.

Please send a cheque or postal order (no currency) and allow 60p for postage and packing for the first book plus 25p for the second book and 15p for each additional book ordered up to a maximum charge of £1.90 in UK.

B.F.P.O. customers please allow 60p for the first book, 25p for the second book plus 15p per copy for the next 7 books, thereafter 9p per book.

Overseas customers, including Eire, please allow £1.25 for postage and packing for the first book, 75p for the second book, and 28p for each subsequent title ordered.

NAME (Block Letters)...

ADDRESS ....

....